THE MONEY THERAPIST

·THE·
MONEY
THERAPIST

A Woman's Guide to
Creating a Healthy Financial Life

MARCIA BRIXEY

SEAL PRESS

The Money Therapist
A Woman's Guide to Creating A Healthy Financial Life

Copyright © 2008 by Marcia Brixey

Page 161: Reprint from *Smart Women Finish Rich* by David Bach, copyright © 1999. Used by permission of Broadway Books, a division of Random House, Inc.

Published by
Seal Press
A Member of the Perseus Books Group
1700 Fourth Street
Berkeley, California 94710

Library of Congress Cataloging-in-Publication Data

Brixey, Marcia.
The money therapist : a woman's guide to managing money and creating a healthy financial life / By Marcia Brixey.
p. cm.
ISBN-13: 978-1-58005-216-0
ISBN-10: 1-58005-216-9
1. Women—Finance, Personal. 2. Finance, Personal. 3. Budgets, Personal. I. Title. II. Title: Woman's guide to managing money and creating a healthy financial life. III. Title: Guide to managing money and creating a healthy financial life. IV. Title: Managing money and creating a healthy financial life.

HG179.B742 2008
332.0240082—dc22
2007039520

Cover design by Gia Giasullo
Interior design by Megan Cooney
Distributed by Publishers Group West
Printed in the USA

This book is dedicated to my wonderful husband, Steve.
Thank you for your love, patience, and support.

CONTENTS

Get Out of the Red and Into the Black

Believe it or not, I already know a lot about you. I know you are not alone in your money challenges or in your feelings of ignorance and confusion about financial issues. I know you sometimes feel hopeless and overwhelmed by economic pressures. And I know you have a strong desire to educate yourself about money and take the steps needed to resolve your situation and create a healthy financial future for yourself and your family.

So how can I know this about you? Because I've been educating women about their finances for several years now, and I listen to the same story with different verses every day. Stories of women who allowed their husbands to control their money and drive them into mountainous debt. Stories of women left in a panicky financial crisis after a divorce or the death of their partner. Stories of women who have overspent themselves into a deep, dark debt pit. Stories of women who've never been taught how to manage their money and who are clueless about using credit wisely. Women who are afraid someone will discover that they're a fraud, that they don't have their finances together at all.

When it comes to money, we tend to think we need to know everything and be perfect before we take any action. So many of the women I've talked to just do nothing at all. This is *not* a good thing, because when it comes to money, the longer you wait, the less time you have on your side. The more you procrastinate, the more money you have to invest to catch up. If a twentysomething woman invests 10 percent of her gross income regularly, she should have enough to live comfortably in her retirement. But the fortysomething woman must invest twice as much, or 20 percent of her gross income, to catch up and enjoy the same financial security.

I've also met many women who are paralyzed by fear. One fifty-six-year-old woman had never requested and reviewed her credit reports because she was afraid of what she would find. Another woman, deep in debt, was scared to death to write down all the debt, afraid of what she would discover. And then there are the women who never open their mail because they don't want to know what they owe. All of these women have succumbed to the financial fallout of denial.

The good news is that it's all fixable. No matter how towering your debts appear, no matter how jammed into a corner you feel, you'll learn in this book exactly what measures to take to dig yourself out. I promise you it will be a journey of self-discovery and illumination, and if you take the steps outlined in these chapters, you'll arrive on the other side of your chaos, financially fit and smiling.

You need only to examine a few statistics to understand why it's important to become educated on financial issues and begin planning your future now. Between raising children and taking care of parents, women lose an average of 14.7 years from the workplace. A woman who's out of the workforce for just one year must work five years to recover lost income, pension coverage, and promotion opportunities. With the divorce rate holding steady at 50 percent and the average age of widowhood at fifty-eight, plus the fact that women live seven to ten years longer than men, the reality is that if you aren't already, at some point you are likely to become solely responsible for your financial security. According to the 2000 Census, women are more than four times more likely than men to be widowed. And 80 percent of women living in poverty were not poor before their husbands died.

According to Women Investing in Security and Education, more women file for bankruptcy than graduate from college, only 34 percent of women have some type of retirement account, the median debt for women has doubled in recent years, and 40 percent of the average woman's income goes to serve mortgage debt.

Women are by nature caregivers and nurturers. We take care of our children, husbands, partners, grandchildren, and parents— and don't forget the family pets! We take care of everyone but ourselves. I think it's because we've been programmed to give to others first and wait to see if there's anything left over for us. For years I thought I was selfish if I did something for myself. It took forever to get past that feeling of selfishness. It didn't change until I read this definition: *Selfish is when you are not doing something someone else wants you to do*. Does that resonate with you? When you're on an airplane, the flight attendants tell you that in case of emergency, put the oxygen mask on yourself first and then help someone else. It's the same with finances. You need to make sure your financial house is in good shape before you can help someone else. Why can't we take care of ourselves and still give generously to others? I believe it's time to respect yourself, be a little selfish (meaning self-sufficient!), and invest in yourself. Give yourself permission to learn the language of money. Skip the financial fallout of denial and embrace your finances. Create your own financial fate. By making that investment now, you'll have a much better quality of life—both financially and personally—in the years ahead.

A ROAD MAP FOR THE JOURNEY

I've arranged this book into ten action categories (chapters two through eleven) to keep you from getting overwhelmed. Read them at your own pace; there is no wrong way to do this work. You may find you want to review some chapters again and again. In fact, you may think you're done "remodeling" one area of your financial house, only to realize months later there is still more to do. This is the normal process of growth and change. Be patient with yourself.

As Vikki, a woman who attended one of my forums, put it, "What I know about my own style of learning is that I need to just expose myself to information over and over, and eventually all the tumblers fall into place and I *get it*."

All along the way you'll read the inspiring success stories of women who've made the journey already. In the first chapter I'll share my own saga of financial awakening, so you'll see that I've been there too.

In Chapter Two you'll learn why it's important to create a personal financial plan based on your personal values and goals. I'll provide you with the steps to determine those goals.

Chapter Three will show you the importance of getting your finances organized and exactly how to do it. You'll see how to create a personal inventory and what you should do with it once you have one. Then you'll learn many different ways to further your education about money. And finally, I'll help you develop a personalized plan of action for financial fitness.

Chapter Four will help you understand exactly where all your money goes—and how to get a lot of it back. It's filled with innovative ways to hang onto more of the money you earn, plus creative yet thrifty ideas for giving.

In Chapter Five we tackle the biggie—you'll learn once and for all how to get out from under your debts. I'll reveal lots of tricks to finesse your situation and warn you of dangerous pitfalls to avoid.

Chapter Six demystifies credit reports and credit scores. You'll learn why you must have three reports, how to interpret them, and most important, how lenders use these reports to determine your financial future. I'll show you exactly how banks and other lenders weigh various aspects of your financial picture, and I'll explain precisely what steps to take to resolve problems with your reports and to improve your credit score.

In Chapter Seven you'll learn about the increasingly common problem of identity theft. I'll explain how it happens and how to protect yourself and your family. I've also included information on what to do if you do become a victim of this crime.

By the time you reach Chapter Eight, you'll be ready to start looking beyond correcting past mistakes and organizing your present-day life. I'll teach you why you need to prepare for whatever the future holds and how to do it rather painlessly. I bet you'll even get excited about making your money work harder for you so you don't have to work so hard yourself.

In Chapter Nine you'll learn the importance of being prepared for the unexpected—death, disability, and natural disasters—all the things we hate to talk or even think about. I'll give you some tips on how you can protect yourself, your family, and your belongings.

Chapter Ten focuses on the types of financial help available to you—you'll learn how to assess various professionals and determine which ones you might want to consult. You'll find checklists for choosing a bank, an insurance company, a mortgage broker, a financial adviser, and a real estate agent.

By this point you are fast becoming a money expert! You've left the red ink of the debt column far behind, and your finances are firmly in the profitable, black column of your ledger. All that's left in Chapter Eleven is to determine your net worth and then to consider sharing your financial education with friends, family, and beyond. Passing on this gift of financial understanding to your children—and even your parents—can be the biggest blessing in this whole journey. It's the big payoff, when you realize you've become a role model for those around you and can celebrate your victory over financial chaos.

So join me on this expedition into financial knowledge, as I first divulge my own learning curve—complete with dips and dives but finally with a triumphant upswing.

ONE

Are You Living in a House of Cards?

How I put a solid foundation under my teetering financial house

Little did I realize when I began my journey to financial fitness that it would provide me with opportunities to live my dream and passion. Yet that's exactly what happened.

As a young girl, I envied the family across the street in my hometown of Visalia, California, because they had so many possessions: flashy new cars, a pool in the backyard, lots of lovely new clothes, and so on. My wise mother explained that things weren't always what they appeared to be and cautioned that perhaps the family went into debt to pay for their shiny baubles. I've never forgotten that conversation with her.

My husband and I recently met a new couple at the golf course. As they walked out to their car, which was a spiffy BMW, I thought, *They must be really well off financially.* I had to stop and remind myself, *Maybe they're financially secure or maybe they're just in debt.* The next time you look at someone who appears to be financially secure, remember things aren't always what they appear to be. We're a nation of spenders—trying to keep up with the Joneses.

Some years back, after attending several financial conferences for women and reading a couple of books, I decided it was time to get our financial house in order. On the plus side of our ledger, my husband and I earned good salaries, paid our bills on time, fully funded our company retirement plan, and had excellent credit. But in the debit column, we carried a $10,000 credit card balance we just couldn't get paid off. We had also failed to set aside money in savings for emergencies, we had no individual retirement accounts (IRAs), and we didn't protect ourselves or our assets with wills.

Yes, from all outward appearances we were a couple who had it all together financially. But the truth was, we didn't really have our financial house in order. We were what I would call "financial frauds." I'm sharing this because I want you to realize that there are many pretenders out there. You're not alone!

I began by writing a financial action plan, which included paying off our credit card debt, establishing emergency and contingency funds, opening an IRA, and meeting with an attorney to write our wills. During the next few years we plodded our way through the plan.

The first thing we did was call our credit card company to request a lower interest rate. We were surprised when they said, "Yes" and reduced our interest rate by 6 percent! We made sacrifices so we could make large payments on the credit card until it was paid off, which took almost two years. What an incredible sense of freedom and empowerment we felt to be free of credit card debt! We also opened our emergency fund in a money market account and funded it through automatic deductions from our paychecks. Every time we got a raise or cost of living adjustment we increased our deduction.

Suze Orman's book *The Nine Steps to Financial Freedom* was a big inspiration and taught me to save my money regularly and automatically—I opened an IRA and funded it by cutting back our cable television to basic service. I tucked the $30 a month we saved into my IRA. And I didn't miss the Home and Garden channel one bit!

OPPORTUNITIES SOMETIMES KNOCK VERY LOUDLY

During that time, I was working for the Social Security Administration as a public relations specialist, and I became passionate about issues surrounding women and their money. I was responsible for women's issues, which provided me the opportunity to attend many financial conferences for women. I also spoke to women's groups about the importance of Social Security and of having pensions and savings to ensure a financially secure retirement.

I believe that everything happens in life for a reason, and that there are lessons to be learned from every situation—good or bad. I always ask myself: *What's the lesson to be learned from this situation?* In January 2001, I encountered some difficult issues in my personal life, which taught me several extremely valuable lessons. For more than a year I struggled before coming to terms with the realization I was no longer happy or satisfied with my job. I wondered what was wrong with me. I questioned how I could dislike the best job I'd ever had—a job with a good salary, excellent benefits, and a great office. It just wasn't sensible to retire before I turned fifty-five, which was eight years away. So I kept going to work—miserable and unhappy.

This passage from *Oprah* magazine was very helpful to me at that time:

Gratitude comes easily when our lives are in order—when the bills are paid, the children are behaving and our health is good. But our challenges are what bring the chance for transformation. And it is during our deepest pain that we can be most grateful, because we know our hardship will deliver a lesson that redefines our character. As you practice gratitude, give thanks not only for what you have, but also for what you've escaped. When difficulties arise, ask yourself "What is the lesson for me in this?" And when you give thanks in the midst of your trial, know that you're becoming your finest.

One day I woke up and wondered where Marcia was. What had happened to me? Yes, physically I was there, but where was the inner, emotional, spiritual me? I finally realized how incredibly unhappy I was. It was almost impossible to name anything in my life that made me happy, except for my wonderful friends and husband. For several weeks I strained to maintain my daily life and routines, but my life was crumbling all around me.

I lost a little more of my composure with each passing day. I tried everything I could think of to keep going, but it just didn't work. I went to see a counselor, and it helped a little. But any patience I had for the stresses of my job was gone.

I can still vividly remember the day I went to work crying nonstop. After listening to a voice mail message from my boss, I completely lost it and knew it was time to take care of *me*. I went home and made a doctor's appointment. People are put in our paths for a reason. My guardian angel that day was a nurse named Marie Bailey. Marie gave me the permission I needed to take care of myself. She told me to take three weeks off work and spend time doing things I loved and to take care of Marcia.

During that three-week period I spent an incredible amount of time reading inspirational books, journaling, and reading my entries from the past year. Finally I realized I had arrived at a different place in my life. I was forty-six years old—this wasn't a dress rehearsal! I identified with something Karen Dinesen says in the film *Out of Africa*: "My biggest fear was that I would come to the end of my life and discover that I lived someone else's dream." Things that were vital to me a year earlier were no longer important to me. My job no longer felt like a career; instead, it was just a way to make a living. It was the best job I ever had, but like everything else, it had changed.

After about a week at home, I read a quote: "Our purpose in life is to find our gift, perfect it and give it back to others" (author unknown). As Oprah would say, that was my "Aha" moment. Immediately I knew my gift was teaching women the importance of financial fitness. But even after my "Aha" moment, I was still afraid of my own future. This is what I wrote in my journal that day:

> I am already wavering on my thoughts of taking early retirement and reaching out to women. I'm sure it's fear of the unknown and risking my secure retirement. It's a terrible place to dwell—fear. I hope I can come to grips with it and move on, if that's what I am supposed to do.

A few days later I wrote:

> I realize my decision to take the early retirement opportunity and move on is the right decision. I've been working up the courage for months. My desire has never wavered. Only fear and waiting to know when the time was right have kept me at work. This opportunity is a gift, and I'm not going to miss my chance to embark on a new adventure!

To make that decision to step into my authentic self, I reread my journal for the previous nine months. What I discovered amazed me. At least once a week I'd written that I wanted to provide women a place to empower themselves, connect with other women, and learn about becoming financially secure. I wrote that I hoped I would have the courage to take this step. My journal was filled with my desire to retire early if offered the opportunity.

I began to recognize the pervasive fear that was holding me back. I took heart from something Eleanor Roosevelt wrote:

> You gain strength, courage and confidence by every experience in which you really stop to look fear in the face. You must do the thing you think you cannot do.

After three weeks at home I returned to work, and I immediately informed my boss that I planned to take early retirement. What a relief! I began living my dream and passion to educate women on financial fitness when I retired on August 3, 2002, and founded Money Wi$e Women. Making the decision to retire early—and knowing we could afford it because we were financially secure—was the most powerful decision I've ever made. And it all began when I decided it was time to get our financial house in order, wrote a financial action plan, and followed it.

And I'll show you how to do the same!

Here's a success story that's sure to inspire you. Kristen is a young urban professional who, like a lot of her peers, was living way beyond her means. She was accruing debt without much regard for the consequences—until the day she decided to get her financial act together.

· PROFIT FROM HER STORY ·

Kristen says:
Budget is not a four-letter word!

"A year ago September I put myself on a budget. It was extremely painful. Looking back, I had never, ever lived within my means. So the first two to three months were really hard as I grappled with what I *really* needed to live on. By January I was doing well—not incurring any more debt *and* paying off what I had already spent.

"But in July, my income declined because of a setback with an unexpected delinquent account in our business. Keeping the business solvent was extremely important, so I reduced my income by $833 a month ($10,000 net annually) to cover the shortfall.

▶

> "Here's the incredible thing: Because I was so diligent about my budget, I was able to handle getting $833 less a month. There was a time when this would have been a disaster. The only impact was that I couldn't pay down the debt as fast, so I figured with this setback it would take me two years to complete.
>
> "Yet by November, with the money I had allocated to debt reduction, I was 100 percent free of consumer debt. In just over one year I eliminated nearly $15,000 in debt that I had been lugging around! When I first started my budget, it was hard to imagine this day—and how on earth I would ever get this worked out. Now I've taken the money I allotted to debt reduction and put it in a savings account."

MY GOALS FOR YOU

I want you to get your financial house in order so you will have the ability to make a variety of choices whenever opportunities present themselves. One example might be losing your job. Perhaps you'd like to go back to school, or you want to start your own business. If you're submerged in debt with no savings or retirement fund, you'll be worried about how you're going to survive financially. But if your financial house is in order and you're financially secure, opportunities will present themselves like chocolate delicacies at a buffet.

As you progress on your journey to achieve financial fitness, you'll feel not only a sense of accomplishment, but also a sense of power. I'm behind you all the way!

Take time now to determine why you want to get your financial house in order. Have you created an emergency fund? Do you have to borrow money to pay for your car when it breaks down?

Are you scrimping by, paycheck to paycheck? Are you drowning in credit card debt? Do you have an IRA? Is your family protected with a will? Do you understand your credit report? Do you simply find the entire subject of money daunting? These are just a few jolts to your money mind, and the answers may reveal why you need to get your financial house in order. Determine your personal reasons and write them down here.

> I want to put my financial house in order because:
>
> _____
> _____
> _____
> _____
> _____
> _____
> _____
> _____
> _____
> _____

· PROFIT FROM HER STORY ·

Annette says:
Sooner is better than later!

"After a picture postcard proposal in front of the Eiffel Tower (to which I said, "Yes," of course!) I soon realized I was going to have to fully reveal myself to my fiancé, Jeff. We were going

▶

▶

to join our incomes, finances, and expenses—and my debts. While Jeff didn't have any debt, I had student loans and credit card debt that had accrued while I completed two degrees. Although I have a good credit score and have paid all my bills in a timely manner, the thought of laying out all my statements and discussing minimum payments with Jeff was daunting.

"However, Jeff helped me prepare by creating budget spreadsheets in Excel, which helped me calculate a debt reduction plan. Next, I arranged current statements of bills and prepared for our discussion. It may not have been the best date night, but with a small box of chocolates and clear heads, we reviewed the balances, minimum payments, and interest rates for all my outstanding debts. By laying it all out on the table, we got it out in the open and were able to decide on the best strategy for our situation.

"I hope that other young couples embarking on the big step of marriage will consider getting their finances in order as a requirement for their new partnership. Although I felt exposed, this is clearly one partnership that needs to have clear communication and open discussion to succeed. It's comforting to know Jeff and I are on the right track toward creating order in our financial house."

I wish all women could be as smart about money as Annette and build their lives on such a solid foundation. Unfortunately, many of us don't, and in this book you'll read about those women too, along with inspiring stories of solutions. Kelley is a classic case, a fortysomething mom who had been in moderate denial about finances until she attended a financial seminar. For those readers who think it must take a long time to get your affairs in order, read what Kelley accomplished in just two months.

· PROFIT FROM HER STORY ·

Kelley says:
I didn't want to waste another minute!

"Money and money management used to be something I thought of like doing windows—give them a good cleaning inside and out once a year, and quick interior cleanings when something got on them; otherwise I left the curtains closed.

"I had started a 401(k) at a previous employer but never rolled it out. I have a traditional IRA and had intentions of making deposits to it but never did. I knew enough about my husband's money, I told myself. After attending a financial conference, I took a new look at my finances—my windows. I realized that windows have a purpose: to give me perspective, protection from the weather, and to work for me. I still have to attend to them and sometimes even replace, repair, or upgrade them. I'm proud of the view through my windows now. They look great now that I threw out those heavy old curtains.

"For me, the most important element of the conference was that it's women teaching women. I listened to a woman speak of losing her husband unexpectedly and the challenges she faced. It was enough to shock me into reality. The very night after attending the conference, I felt empowered to go to my husband, and I said, "Honey, we need to talk." Fortunately, it was a conversation my husband had longed to have. He wanted me to participate in the household finances and financial decisions. It felt as if someone pulled the wool back from my eyes and made me look closely at that window. Money was working me, not working for me. So since that night, I have stepped up and taken my rightful place in my financial house. Now, not only am I a wife, a mother, and a homemaker, I'm also my own money manager.

►

> ▶
>
> "We have leveraged our mortgage to buy two rental properties, which brings in about $600 in passive income a month. We have an appointment with an attorney to plan our estate; we've had the uncomfortable conversations and made decisions. I know what my credit score is. I know what's in my credit reports. I have a plan to pay off my car loan and my student loan in less than three months, and then I'll be debt free. I have requested a rollover of my employer's 401(k) into an account that I can manage myself. I know where my husband's money is, and I can get to it if something happens. I know how much we pay in monthly utilities and how to pay them. I know our insurance plans. I am learning about mortgages, buying investment properties, and property management."

And Kelley accomplished all that in just two months! Get prepared to take action and get your financial problems under your control. As you read the inspirational stories in this book from women just like you, I hope you'll see it is possible to dig your way out of even the deepest hole. One of my favorite quotes from JoAnn Contorno sums up my journey: "Dreams become goals when you decide to do the work to make them come true." The rest of this book is about passing on my message of financial responsibility to you and challenging you to meet your own goals. So let's get started!

TWO

Determine Your Goals and Write an Action Plan

How to design the floor plan of your financial house

Chapter Goals for You
· Get clarity about your goals
· Write them down
· Make sure they are SMART goals
· Learn to understand prosperity

THE IMPORTANCE OF GOAL SETTING

I believe determining your goals and putting them in writing is crucial if you want to succeed in achieving financial fitness. To attain financial independence, you need to create a personal financial plan based on your personal values and goals. Some questions to ask yourself:

- Imagine you could do or have anything you wanted. What would you do with your life if you were financially independent and didn't have to work or worry about money?

- Imagine that your doctor told you that you had only three to five years to live. What would you do with the time left to you?

- Write your own eulogy. What do you want to accomplish before you die, and how do you want people to remember you?

- Take time to fantasize, daydream, and think outside the box. According to Brian Tracy, author of *Goals! How to Get Everything You Want—Faster Than You Ever Thought Possible*, "the biggest single obstacle to setting goals is self-limiting beliefs." Pretend you're the CEO of your own life. Determine what's most important to you.

Maria Nemeth, author of *The Energy of Money*, says that people often confuse goals with tasks. "Tasks are what should or ought to be done. They clear the way for your goals. A key for determining a task versus a goal is whether you'll be relieved when it's done. When a task is completed, you feel relief." It's like when you write a To Do list and mark a nice big line through each task as you complete it. I don't know about you, but I get so much more done when I'm working off a list. It's always a pleasure to cross the task off my To Do List.

Here's an example of my goals and tasks. One year my goal was Claiming My Power: to love my appearance, feel like a million bucks, and wear chic, sassy clothes. The tasks I committed to do in order to accomplish this included: working out at the gym at least three days a week, Pilates lessons twice a week, walking with my husband and our dogs five days a week, attending Weight Watchers meetings and cooking delicious low-fat meals, saying goodbye to my daily glass of wine, and getting an image consultation. I also included some rewards for my accomplishments: For every ten pounds I lost, I treated myself to a facial and for every month I accomplished my exercise goals, I treated myself to a pedicure.

While the focus of this book is your financial goals, this advice applies to all kinds of goals. Having goals and a purpose will give you passion and a reason to get up and get on with your day. But remember to set goals that you can achieve, and make sure the goals you set are truly your own—don't make a goal that someone else wants you to accomplish. When you've completed a goal, you'll feel joy, so take time to revel in it and congratulate yourself. I know from personal experience that if you keep your goals in your head, you probably won't be successful. Take time to determine your goals, and then your goals *must* be put in writing. Putting your goals in writing crystallizes them and gives them more force. If you keep your goals only in your head, you'll forget them. We keep so much information in our heads that it's hard to keep it all straight. I can walk from one end of the house to another and forget why I'm there. Determining your goals will:

- Provide you with a sense of meaning, purpose, and direction
- Help you gain clarity and decide what's important
- Determine what is important to you versus what is relevant
- Motivate you to achieve success
- Help you achieve more
- Help you focus
- Increase your motivation to succeed
- Improve your self-confidence

WHAT ARE YOUR FINANCIAL GOALS?

Determine your financial goals, make them specific, and put them in writing with an anticipated completion date. If you're married or partnered, I recommend each of you determine your financial goals individually. Then get together to compare and discuss the goals you've set. Each of you may have a completely different list, which will require discussion and possibly compromise in setting joint financial goals.

The acronym SMART is a simple method to use to determine your goals.

Specific

Make your goals clear, precise, and positive. Be sure to set only positive goals for yourself. For example, don't write: "Never use my credit cards again;" instead, write: "Use my credit cards wisely and sparingly." Write your goal as a positive statement rather than a negative statement:

> Positive statement: I will save to buy a home.
> Negative statement: I will not spend money.

This may sound woo-woo to some of you, but I've seen this in action, again and again. Using positive language attracts positive outcomes, situations, and people into your life. If you tell yourself you can't spend money, you'll be in deprivation mode. And your monkey mind will keep asking, "Why can't I spend any money?" Pretty soon, you'll be out spending money even though you made a goal not to spend.

Measurable

Determine how you will measure your success. For example: "I will contribute $100 per month to my IRA" or "I will request and review my credit report this week." Both of these goals can easily be measured.

Attainable

Make your goals a stretch. Set goals that you can achieve. Don't make it too easy, but don't make it too difficult either. Make it something that is worth working toward, yet attainable. For example, "I'm saving $500 per month toward the down payment on a house."

Relevant

Ask yourself if your goal is relevant to your financial intentions, and make your goal relevant to what matters to you, what you want to achieve, what lights your fire and gives you joy. Don't make a goal that someone else wants you to accomplish. It *must* be your goal alone, unless you're married or partnered and working on your financial goal-setting together.

Time-based

Creating a timeline for accomplishing your goals and setting a deadline are absolute musts. Anchor your goal in time; know that an idea isn't a goal until you set a date for it. For example, complete a household inventory. Your goal statement could be, "At least once a month I will inventory a room in my home to ensure my inventory is completed in twelve months." Time-based goals create their own clarity and power. A goal without a deadline is like saying to yourself, "I'll get around to it one day." Once you determine a due date, you've made a commitment to yourself, and your subconscious will begin putting the pieces in place to make it happen.

My financial goals are:

_____
_____
_____
_____
_____
_____
_____
_____
_____
_____
_____
_____
_____
_____
_____
_____
_____
_____

Once you complete a goal, congratulate yourself and then go on to the next one. To succeed with your goals, consider these tips:

- Keep records. I kept a journal for six months in preparation for my participation in the Susan G. Komen Three-Day Breast Cancer Walk. I noted my daily activities, which included walking, exercising, and eating. Journaling helped keep me on track, and I'm proud to say it was an amazing and life-changing experience!

- Reward yourself when you achieve success. Too often we beat ourselves up over setbacks. We let our monkey mind chatter on, giving us negative feedback. Most of us would never say the things we say to ourselves to someone else. So don't forget to celebrate your success—both the steps you've taken and the progress you've made.

During the period in my life when I was working for the Social Security Administration, I didn't have any meaningful goals. My goals were going on vacation, spending time with my husband, getting a promotion at work, and so on. I realized I was just in a survival mode, which wasn't a bad thing, but eventually I discovered I wasn't living the joyful, purposeful life I was meant to live. During the past five years, I've redefined my personal and business goals numerous times. I have used a life coach to help me, because it's almost impossible for me to get quiet enough by myself to think about my goals. I attribute this to my personality and to being a woman who has spent many, many years multitasking and never sitting still. (I always have something to do, even when I'm sitting in front of the television at night.) Obviously there is no one-size-fits-all way to get motivated, but the good news is that every one of us can find ways to focus on our goals and get inspired in a way that's perfectly tailored to the needs of our unique personalities.

ARE YOU READY TO TAKE ACTION?

I challenge you to determine your action step commitments. In the Appendix, I've compiled a list of all the action steps I recommend throughout the book. These are tasks for helping you achieve financial fitness and ultimately attain your goals. It's an extensive list that includes a variety of tasks, some of which are relatively simple and can be accomplished fairly easily and quickly. Other tasks are more complex and time consuming. I recommend you select one, two, or more action steps that you intend to accomplish in the next sixty days. Although these are tasks and not goals, my guess is that you'll feel some joy and even pride once you've accomplished them.

I commit to taking the following
action steps in the next sixty days:

_____
_____
_____
_____
_____
_____
_____
_____
_____
_____
_____
_____
_____
_____
_____
_____
_____
_____

· PROFIT FROM HER STORY ·

Corey says:
Writing down my goals worked!

"I set up a list of five financial commitments for October, November, and December, and I have so far been meeting them. I just opened my first Roth IRA and helped my husband redo his plan. (I'm twenty-three, and my employer does not match retirement accounts.) I have been tracking our expenses for the last four months. We are working on a budget. I asked for a raise and received it."

LIVING A LIFE OF PROSPERITY

Most people include some version of prosperity in their financial goals. Many people define prosperity as the summation of their tangible possessions: their careers or positions at work, education or degrees they've earned, where they live, cars they drive, schools their children attend, vacations they take, and even clothes and accessories they wear. They also associate prosperity with having an abundance of money.

What is prosperity? According to Webster's dictionary, prosperity is "the condition of being successful or thriving; *esp:* economic well-being." Shakti Gawain, author of *Creating True Prosperity*, describes prosperity as the "experience of having plenty of what we truly need and want in life, material and otherwise." According to Ellen Peterson, author of *Choosing Joy, Creating Abundance,* "Prosperity is not what you have or how much you make; it's actually how you think." And Maria Nemeth, author of *The Energy of Money*, writes, "Prosperity comes when you participate fully in *every* aspect of your life."

In June 2003, I attended Oprah's "Live Your Best Life Tour." Oprah said that life speaks to you first in whispers, and that's your intuition. If you're not paying attention, life gets a little louder or taps you on your shoulder. If you're still not paying attention, life hits you on the head with a metaphorical brick. If you're still ignoring life's speaking to you, a brick wall will fall on you. And finally, if you're still not paying attention, an earthquake will grab it.

Prosperity is created by setting intentions. Intentions create thoughts. Thoughts create choices. Choices create different outcomes or actions. Are you ready to live a life of prosperity? Start by taking time to be quiet and listen to yourself. Most women have trouble getting quiet because we're multitaskers and busy taking care of everyone but ourselves. But it's crucial to carve some quiet time for yourself. I've learned how to do that for myself. I'm not good about journaling regularly, but I've discovered that walking my dogs daily and listening to music on my iPod gets my creative juices flowing. When I have a little more time, I read an inspirational or motivational book, or I spend time creating handmade cards. You need to discover what works for you.

Think about what your intentions are and take time to get to know yourself better. Spend time excavating your inner thoughts and writing them down—what makes you happy and what motivates you. Know that life isn't happening without you. You're in the driver's seat; you're in charge! You are responsible for your choices. Align your life with what's important to you, and you'll be on the road to living a life of prosperity.

If you're ready to live a life of prosperity ask yourself:

- What does prosperity mean to me?
- What actions and choices can I make to create prosperity in my life?
- What are the areas where I intend to make new choices?

To set accurate financial goals for yourself, it's important to base them on the things you truly value. Circle the words that reflect your values—not your parents', friends', or society's, but the values that are important to *you*—or add your own values.

- Spiritual fulfillment
- Health
- Family and/or friends
- Helping people
- Financial security
- Making a difference

- Influence

- Creativity

- Being the best, an expert in my field

- Having stability in my life

- Adventure

- Excitement

- Independence

- Time

- Travel

- Freedom

- Happiness

- Peace of mind

- Fun

- Security

As you read this book, keep a pad of paper and pen handy. Jot down your goals and the tasks you need to complete to accomplish your goals. Incorporate your values into the goals you set for yourself.

YOU REALLY CAN FIND A WAY OUT— SET GOALS AND KEEP MOVING TOWARD THEM

I love this story of Kit and her family, because it incorporates the whole arc of moving from trouble to triumph through dogged determination. I hope it inspires you too.

· PROFIT FROM HER STORY ·

Kit says:

If I can do it, anyone can!

"My husband and I had been undergoing some financial difficulty for some time. Not long after the birth of our first child, we entered a debt management program. We understood that money would be tight for a long time, but we knew it was the ethical thing to do. About a year ago, when we were close to the end of the program, I started researching ways we could be smarter with our money. The following changes have taken place in my life:

- I found a life coach.
- I reevaluated my principles and beliefs and decided that my current work situation did not serve me. (I had been there eleven years.)
- I found a new job that I love, and I was promoted in my new organization within five months of starting work there.
- I have reengaged with my church and have become an active member.
- We now have short-term and long-term financial plans and insurance in place, including wills.
- My family's finances are stable and more secure than they ever have been.
- We bought a new car (we had previously not been able to fit the whole family into one of our vehicles!).
- My husband and I are now shopping for our first home.

"In short, I have gone from being acceptably surviving to thriving! I am more happy and successful and confident about the future than ever before in my life."

In Chapter Three, we're going to roll up our sleeves and prepare for the work ahead by getting your papers organized. Don't flinch! I'll help you understand what you need to keep and what you can toss, so let's get going.

· THREE ·

Get Organized, Get Educated, and Get Going!

How to clean the attic of your financial house and conquer your chaos

---

Chapter Goals for You

- Learn principles of organizing your money matters
- Sort and then toss or save your financial papers
- Take an inventory of important documents
- Choose action steps for your continuing financial education
- Expand your fiscal understanding
- Develop a personal master plan for getting your finances in order

---

I admit it isn't very glamorous or especially fun to confront the state of your finances by having to organize your records, but it is the foundation of your financial house. Do you want to construct your house on wobbly posts stuck haphazardly into the soil, or do you want to pour concrete into well-built forms for a continuous, solid underpinning? I thought so!

DO SOME FINANCIAL HOUSECLEANING

A good way to start your journey to financial fitness is to organize and clear your clutter. Clutter sucks the energy out of you and prevents good things from happening and coming your way. Organizing your financial records will help you determine how much money you have and how much you owe. You will also feel a sense of freedom, power, and accomplishment. If your financial records are in a mess, take pity on family or friends who might be called upon to deal with them. Organize for their benefit, if nothing else!

Years ago I had a supervisor who explained her Mack truck theory. It goes something like this: If you were run over by a Mack truck on the way to work, could someone come into your home and find all your financial paperwork? If not, then it's time to get rid of your clutter and organize your records.

What records, you may ask? Start looking in the piles of paper we all tend to accumulate and the inbox so buried in paper that you may have forgotten there's a box beneath it. You may have stowed papers pertaining to your car in your glove box. You may actually have some important documents in a safe deposit box. (Way to go!) Or you may just have a kitchen drawer where you stuff official-looking papers. Scientists have recently discovered that we have an enormous number of genes in common with the lowly mouse. I'm betting it's also true of the relentless pack rat!

If you can't find your vital records (e.g., birth certificates, marriage certificate, citizenship paperwork, etc.), visit www.firstgov.gov to determine how and where to submit your request for replacements. You may not need these documents right away, but they are usually required when you're requesting a passport, filing for disability or retirement benefits, and so on.

Begin by buying a two-drawer file cabinet, plastic bin, file crate, or one of those file boxes with a lid and handle. Also buy plenty of file folders to fit. You can use different color folders for different categories: green folders for the financial accounts (assets) and red folders for creditors (liabilities), and so on.

Let's get started. Set aside several hours of quiet time along with plenty of space to organize your piles. The kitchen or dining room table usually works perfectly. Have empty file folders on hand, along with scrap paper for notes. You'll also want a trash can and box for shredding nearby. I don't recommend you spend the time shredding while you're in the process of organizing. You can shred later.

Determine the organizational categories you plan to use, but make them logical to ensure that anyone can figure them out. My folders are labeled by account name: UTILITIES, MORTGAGE, HEALTH INSURANCE, AUTO INSURANCE, HOMEOWNERS INSURANCE, CREDIT CARDS, PAY STUBS, and so on. Review the monthly spending plan summary in the Appendix for a complete list of categories. Keeping the folders in alphabetical order makes them easy to find. (Don't put the dog's records under the name of your vet. That could change; plus, someone else might not *know* who your vet is. File them under Missy. Or Scruffy. You get my point.)

Collect all your financial papers, including those already filed, unopened statements and bills, and bills waiting to be paid. Next, sort through your paperwork, placing it in the appropriate files.

Have a file for questionable items that you can go back and review later. If you have bills to be paid, pay them before you finish. You have a number of ways to organize your bills awaiting payment—in a small labeled folder, small basket, or organizer. Use whatever works best for you. If you try one way and it's not working, try another. Another idea for making bill-paying easier is to call your creditors and ask them to adjust your due date to come right after your paydays. You can also use Microsoft Money or Quicken to organize your finances and remind you of the payment due dates (more on that later).

Clear your financial clutter

Now you're ready to reduce the piles and relieve some chaos by getting rid of outdated paperwork. Shred any papers you're not keeping that contain personal information: Social Security number, date of birth, account numbers, and so on. Identity thieves poke through trash bins and dumpsters for personal information so they can steal your identity. Don't throw out paperwork you may need for tax purposes. According to the IRS, the general rule of thumb for both personal and business papers is seven years. The IRS can audit you three years from the date you file your taxes, but since there are so many exceptions, play it safe and hold your paperwork for seven years. Paperwork you might consider tossing, *if* it isn't needed for tax reasons, includes:

- Old automobile, homeowners, and health insurance policies
- Outdated warranties and instruction manuals
- Utility statements
- Credit card statements—keep through the current year
- Bank and credit union statements
- Mutual fund reports
- Pay stubs (only through the current year)—keep the last pay stub for past years (should contain year-to-date information).
- Computer software boxes (you need to keep the product key, which can be found on the box, CD case, or on the product itself)

If you're in doubt about whether you need to save something, consult your accountant or tax preparer. Or if there's a chance it might be needed, then save it. Tax records can be sealed in large envelopes, clearly marked, and put in a storage area other than the prime real estate next to your desk.

Inventory your financial records

The next step is to prepare an inventory of your financial records by summarizing the name, address, phone number, and account number(s) for the following items, using the inventory of assets and liabilities chart provided in the Appendix. This gives you a starting point and makes it easier for your family if something happens to you. It can easily be scanned into your computer and stored on a memory stick or removable disk drive. Make sure several family members know where to find this summary—but since this list also contains virtually everything needed to steal your identity, be careful where you keep it! You can keep it at home in a fireproof box or a safe deposit box, or send it to a trusted family member or friend. Be sure to update it annually.

- Bank, credit union, or money market accounts
- Insurance policies (auto, life, health, disability, long-term care, homeowners, etc.)
- Mortgage and home equity loans
- Automobile loans
- Boat or recreational vehicle loans
- Credit card accounts
- Investments (stocks, mutual funds, bonds, etc.)
- Retirement accounts, IRAs, and so on
- Benefits available through your employer, including contact name and phone number

- Location of your will, durable power of attorney, healthcare directive, living will, trust documents, and so on

- U.S. Savings Bonds, including denomination, serial number, and issue date

- Attorney's name, address, and phone number

Safeguard important documents

You're almost done organizing—just don't delay this critical task. Valuable documents and personal papers should be kept in a fireproof box at home or a safe deposit box at your bank. Most banks charge a nominal fee for safe deposit box rentals. Some documents should be kept at home, because if they're in the safe deposit box and you need them when the financial institution is closed, you'll be out of luck. Valuable documents include:

- Will or living trust (at home)

- Durable power of attorney (at home)

- Durable power of attorney for healthcare (at home)

- Passports (at home)

- Household inventory

- Property deeds: automobile, boat, home, and so on

- Birth certificates for all household members

- Marriage certificate(s)

- Military service records

- Divorce or separation records

- Citizenship or adoption records

- Life insurance policies

- Long-term care insurance policies

- Jewelry appraisals

Next, make a list of what's in your safe deposit box, and add that to the inventory of financial records you started earlier. Give copies to your family and attorney, and be sure to tell your family and executor of your will or living trust where you keep your safe deposit box and key. It doesn't do any good to have your documents in a secure place if no one can find them!

· PROFIT FROM HER STORY ·

Kathie says:
Plan ahead!

"I finished our personal inventory and photos last night and made copies to keep in three different places (our fireproof safe, my mom's house, my sister's house). Then we got my credit report, as well as ones for my husband and his mom. Next I'm finding an appraiser to evaluate all these antiques so I can get our insurance properly adjusted. I also joined an investment club, and I've been putting 10 to 15 percent of each bit of business income into an account—at first into a CD and now into a mutual fund. My husband's mother passed away recently, but one thing I can say is: Thank god for my financial study and the steps I took this past year. We were able to get her will, living will, health directive, and so on in place. It doesn't make this any easier right now, but it certainly will once we work through the shock and grief and have to deal with the logistics of the estate."

TALK IS CHEAP BUT INVALUABLE

Once you've cleared your clutter, emptied those shoe boxes of receipts, and organized your records, you're ready to further your financial education. Women are a community. We talk about our problems, achievements, and successes, and we share ideas and suggestions for overcoming them. We talk about our kids, husbands, partners, bosses, coworkers, parents, even our sex lives, but we won't talk about money. Why? Because it's a taboo subject, and many of us were raised not to talk about it. Then there are the shame and fear factors. We think we're the only ones who don't understand money or who are in credit card debt.

My challenge to you is: *Let's talk about money!* Talk to your family, friends, coworkers, and others who are interested and want to learn. I talked about money to anyone who would listen. I figured if I didn't understand this money stuff, there must be plenty of other women who didn't understand it either. And I discovered I wasn't alone. There's no shame in having credit card debt or not understanding financial topics. I'm not suggesting you reveal all the details about your debt or other financial issues. Perhaps begin the conversation by asking a friend if she has an emergency account, what kind of account it's in, and what interest rate it pays.

You have lots of ways to learn about money. Many women have told me that it's more enjoyable to learn when you have the support of someone else. Find someone who wants to join you on your journey to becoming financially fit. Make an agreement with someone else to learn about finances and money together. Make it fun, and work together to keep each other on point. You don't have to do it alone. Begin to engage in healthy conversations about money. Work together on your action steps, tasks, and goals. Develop an advisory board of people who can assist and support you on your quest for financial fitness.

Starting a book club is a great way to learn about money and finances. When I was still working at the Social Security Administration, I started a book club with fifteen of my coworkers. One of the books we read was *The Nine Steps to Financial Freedom* by Suze Orman.

Every few weeks we met at lunch to discuss a chapter, and then we'd invite financial professionals to come talk about what we'd read. Our speakers included a financial adviser, a mortgage loan officer, a long-term care specialist, and a human resource specialist who educated us on our pension benefits.

Another good way to learn is to attend classes, conferences, seminars, or workshops. Local community colleges offer a variety of financial classes. Watch the newspaper for financial conferences or seminars. Women who have attended my forums and developed a written action plan are making great strides in putting their financial houses in order. Many women repeatedly attend the forums because it usually takes hearing something more than once before it clicks. Think about it—did you learn a foreign language by taking one class? No, you attended lots of classes, read, practiced, and took tests before you became fluent. The same thing applies with money and finances. Learning about money is a process. After all, isn't money like a foreign language?

Ellen says, "I had been contributing to a mutual fund for several years before I fully understood what it was. I had listened to financial experts explain mutual funds and read books, but I just couldn't quite get it. One night I heard a financial adviser on television explain how mutual funds worked, and I finally got it!"

Here's a sampling of some of the other women's comments:

Melissa says, "I am determined to keep reading and learning until the concepts sound like something I've heard before. My self-concept about money and taking care of myself financially is in the infant stage, and I have a lot of fear around money."

Carrie says, "I like to consider myself relatively financially savvy. I've read many, many financial books, and I still learn new things when I attend financial workshops and conferences."

So remember, you're not going to learn everything you know about money by reading one book or attending one class, seminar, or workshop.

The Women's Institute for Financial Education (WIFE) developed Money Clubs, which provides the information and support you need to set your own financial course and for women to learn about money together. You don't have to know much about money to join one of these clubs. All you need is a desire to improve your relationship with money and the willingness to do a little research for your group. For more information on Money Clubs, visit www.MoneyClubs.com.

How about joining or starting an investment club? The Beardstown Ladies made a spectacular success—and a best-selling book—out of theirs. Investment clubs bring a group of interested people together to learn how to invest in various areas. You're actually investing your money together as a group while you're learning. For detailed information, check out the National Association of Investment Corporation at www.betterinvesting.org.

· PROFIT FROM HER STORY ·

Sandra says:
It's up to you to get involved!

"Recently I woke up and realized how little I knew about taking charge of the household finances, because my husband does it all. But I insisted on knowing what's going on, and I've reviewed

▶

---

the records in his checkbook and on his computer. Before, I felt as if I were spying, since he did not openly share this information with me. Now I tell him it's for the good of both of us and for our survival for me to be involved. My husband was planning on retiring in three years, and I discovered our finances were in a mess! But now I've had our property assessed, and I learned we are sitting on a gold mine of land. I learned the true value of real estate and how we can use it. This one bit of knowledge alone will not only clear up our financial mess, but it will also provide for a very comfortable retirement. That is not going too well just yet, but we are working on it. Too much debt is the problem, but I am determined to get it under control. I am also working on purging my house—soon I'll be having one heck of a garage sale!"

LEARNING OPPORTUNITIES

Sherry and her husband, Hank, started playing the Cashflow 101 board game, hosted by a local mortgage company. The game is designed to teach players basic investment skills and how to convert earned income into passive income. Although she's not much of a board game player, Sherry loves to socialize and thought it might lead them to understand real estate investing.

"We are just beginners at ages sixty-three and sixty-five! Since we began playing a few months ago, we've been able to buy a few properties, something we never thought possible. As we introduced ourselves to the other players, each person was asked to tell why he or she was here to play the game. Many had well-defined ideas as to how this would help their investment potential, but I merely said I was there to be supportive of my husband's new hobby. Our hostess then replied that this game had a way of surprising the players and showing them things about their money attitudes that they might not have previously recognized. Halfway through the game, as I struggled to manage my money and properties, I began to feel quite sharklike, in that I *wanted* to buy and sell and acquire and wheel and deal! A money attitude I'd never seen in myself was definitely emerging. We have since played Cashflow 101 several more times, and each time, I meet new people with exciting new ideas, and I find out something about my own abilities to deal with money. This is the first time I have thought money management could be *fun!*"

Another approach is to plan your learning as if it were a college course. Kathie developed an intensive ninety-day plan. She set aside the first thirty minutes of each day to read books on financial issues. Kathie also started a finance journal, which included a list of financial goals. In addition, she's attending classes and taking a personal inventory of her household items, and she has joined an investment and book club. Her ninety-day commitment is a great example of using the SMART goal-setting technique—specific, measurable, attainable, relevant, and time-based.

Many resources are free. Online financial resources are abundant, so why not subscribe to some online newsletters? One excellent example is the Motley Fool, a weekday newsletter that provides market information and articles on financial topics. It's filled with good information that's easy to read and understand. One woman told me she received this newsletter for a couple of years and the only thing she looked at was the Dow Jones and S&P 500 stock market indexes to see if they had gone up or down. Eventually she discovered that a stock market index is simply a statistical indicator of the performance of a particular group of stocks.

HOW TO GET GOING

Several years ago I began my making my New Year's resolutions financially related. Previously, my New Year's resolutions were always weight-related. Each year from January through July I lost weight, but my old habits would gradually return, and by December I gained the weight back. Personally, I had much more success with my financially related resolutions. It was too overwhelming for me to take all my action steps at once, so I started by taking one manageable step at a time, using the list below.

My financial action steps

- Read and talk about money
- Track spending and develop a spending plan
- Pay off credit card debt
- Open an emergency fund
- Fund an IRA for my husband and myself
- Learn about mutual funds, and open an account
- Review my homeowners and automobile insurance policies
- Make an appointment with an attorney to write a will
- Invest in U.S. Savings Bonds through automatic deductions from our paychecks
- Regularly pay extra money on my mortgage
- Make an appointment with a financial adviser

You can do it . . . I know you can!

Review the list of action steps in the Appendix to determine the action steps you intend to take. Break the tasks down into manageable chunks, and then get started. Once you progress to the next step—the educational process—you'll find plenty of reasons to get excited by what you're learning. A real buzz comes from acquiring knowledge that you couldn't get from a dozen half-soy venti lattes!

One good place to start is the Wi$e Up program, which was developed by the U.S. Department of Labor, Women's Bureau. The Wi$e Up program connects Generation X and Y women aged twenty-two to thirty-five with online resources to achieve financial security. The website features an interactive curriculum, suggestions from financial experts, and compelling statistics on women and money. The program also offers monthly, toll-free teleconference calls. For more information, visit the website at www.wiseupwomen.org.

You never know when your newfound money smarts will pay off. Take Denise, for example, who filed for divorce a few years ago. When Denise attended her first asset division meeting, she learned that her husband's proposal was to sell the house, take half the proceeds, pull the kids out of private school, and pay no support payments! Needless to say, she knew better than to sign that.

She has since gotten her files in better order and joined a wonderful divorce support group. She's also handling her credit card more like a debit card, noting each purchase she makes in a register. Denise realizes this is no time to be racking up more debt, and she's well on her way to surviving this life-altering event in a financially sound manner. Pay close attention, though, to her invaluable hindsight.

· PROFIT FROM HER STORY ·

Denise says:
Think everything through really well!

"At the beginning of my divorce, I wanted to keep the house for the sake of the kids, but I'm learning that that is a big mistake

▶

► women make. They keep a house they can't afford, the husband takes off with the rest of the assets (properties, investments, cash), and then the woman can't maintain the house and has to sell it and pay all the taxes and so on, which leaves her on welfare.

"By the time the dust settled, a year later, I realized how complicated our finances had become. I also realized that in the twenty-plus years of my marriage, I was informed of our investments only after the fact, and I wasn't an actual participant. I learned what it meant to not be the primary signer, only the secondary, and that there is a huge difference in power between the two. To this day, I pull up my credit report to find that he still has more control over things that happened in our marriage than I do—for example, property investments and closing bank accounts.

"I am learning through baby steps all the things I should have been paying attention to all along. I let the man handle the complicated issues that I thought were over my head, instead of educating myself on what was going on around me with our investments. Now I'm learning so much about things I should have been on top of—for example: a will, trust funds, retirement, investment accounts and what they contained and in what proportions, real estate investing, mortgages, diversification, as well as other issues that were as simple as learning to dye my own hair and lower my cost from $70 to $7."

Divorce does provide another potential financial sinkhole. Women often want to keep the home they're living in and let the husband keep his retirement benefits. Unfortunately, these aren't always the best decisions. Retirement benefits include company pension and 401(k) plans, federal, state, and local employee retirement plans, medical benefits in retirement, and individual retirement accounts (IRAs). These benefits are often one of the largest assets in divorce situations, and ensuring you get part of your husband's retirement benefits can provide you with financial security later in life.

The Women's Institute for Secure Retirement (www.wiser .heinz.org) is a great resource for information. It also provides a list of seven key questions to ask about pension benefits *before* your divorce is final:

1. Does your husband have more than one pension or retirement plan from his current or previous job?

2. Has your husband worked long enough to earn a legal right to the pension?

3. Do you know how much your husband has earned or "accrued" in pension benefits under each plan?

4. Do you need to have the benefit valued?

5. Do you know what information needs to be in the court order, decree, or property settlement before the pension plan will pay the benefits directly to you?

6. Does the order provide for survivor benefits, so that your benefits can continue if your ex-husband should die first?

7. Does the order clearly specify what amount is to be paid to you?

Visit the Women's Institute for Secure Retirement website for more detailed information.

Now it's time to commit to improving your financial picture. Pick some things you can promise yourself to complete, and perhaps enlist a friend and hold each other to your goals. It doesn't really matter how you begin or what stumbling block you shove out of the way first. Just get going!

Circle the action steps you plan to take in the next sixty days, or write your own action steps.

O Read a book about money or finances

O Read something about money every day

O Talk about money with family and friends

O Get a money buddy—someone to learn about money with and to hold me accountable

O Organize my financial records

O Start or join a book club

O Start or join an investment club

O Take a class on finance

O Attend a financial seminar or workshop

O Start a Money Club using the information provided on www.moneyclubs.com

O Sign up for the Money Wi$e Women newsletter

O Study financial websites

O Subscribe to an online financial newsletter

O Look for learning opportunities in the community

O Read the Money Wi$e Women blog at www.moneywisewomenblog.net

O Other ideas: _____

_____

_____

_____

_____

_____

_____

_____

Also see the Appendix for an inventory worksheet for assets and liabilities that will help you keep track of all your finances, and the Resources section for a list of financial and motivational books and websites.

Now don't you feel better for creating a tidy financial house? I urge you to develop the good habits to keep it that way. In the next chapter, you'll learn how to get in touch with your spending and understand exactly where all your money goes. Find out how to hang on to more of your money and learn about creative ways to trim your spending.

· FOUR ·

Get in Touch with Your Spending

How to find and fix the leaky faucets in your financial house

Chapter Goals for You

- Track every dime you spend
- Analyze your findings
- Identify places to reduce spending
- Pledge to follow your action plan
- Rethink the kinds of gifts you give

IT'S TIME TO CONTROL THE OUTFLOW

Every house needs resources to operate: water, electricity, and sometimes other fuels. For your home to function smoothly, you expect these resources to always be available. It's the same with your financial house. Think of money as energy, and think of spending as draining your resources. If you left the water running day and night and left all the lights and appliances on twenty-four/seven, you'd have some whopping utility bills. Well, spending every dollar you earn—or worse, spending *more* than you earn—has a very high cost too. It means you can't save money for the kids' college fund, your retirement, or even for simple emergencies such as car repairs. Wouldn't you like your money to always be available to you, as easily as you switch on a lamp? Well it can be, and it all starts with reining in your spending.

We're a nation of spenders, and we spend unconsciously for all kinds of reasons. How many of the following reasons for spending can you identify with?

- Retail therapy

- Celebrating

- Impressing others—keeping up with the Joneses

- Thinking *I deserve it*

- Thinking *I earned it*

- Thinking *Why not, I work hard*

- Depression

- Boredom

- Anger

Many of us are living beyond our means, spending more than we earn. And it's no wonder, after we review this list!

What's your money mind-set?

On my financial journey, the very first thing I did was track my spending for a month. I wrote down every penny I spent. After I tracked my spending, I examined my records for ways to trim my spending. One thing I discovered was how much I wasted on my daily latte. *But how,* I wondered, *could I give up my daily social time with my friends at work?*

My solution was simple: I drank regular coffee, which saved me about $2 per day. That was $10 per week, or $40 a month. I still enjoyed a coffee break with my friends, but I was saving money at the same time. After all, until the last decade or so, we all managed to enjoy "ordinary" coffee! That was a fairly painless start.

Eric Tyson, author of *Personal Finance for Dummies,* writes that people fall into one of the following three categories:

- People who spend more than they earn (accumulate debt)

- People who spend all of what they earn (save nothing)

- People who save 2 percent, 5 five percent, 10 percent, or even 20 percent (or more!)

I confess I've dwelt in each of these categories at one point in my life. How about you? Which category do you fit into? You might fit in more than one category, or maybe somewhere in between. It's important to acknowledge your tendencies in both spending and saving, because it gives you a place to start developing your own action plan to achieve financial fitness.

Give yourself a spending reality check

Begin by writing down everything you spend for *at least* fourteen days. Two weeks is long enough to notice trends, but really, if you can keep it up, a month of tracking is ideal.

Try not to spend any differently—just write it all down. You'll probably think twice before buying some things, but the idea is to document how you're actually spending your money now. It's a lot like journaling your food intake for Weight Watchers. What usually happens is that you don't want to write the points down, so you don't eat the food. The same things happen when you track your spending. You become more conscious about what you're spending your money on and often times don't make the purchase.

Take a small notebook or a blank checkbook register, and write down everything you buy with cash, your ATM card, debit card, credit card, check, and so on. My prediction is you'll discover "dollar dribbling"—things you're spending more on than you thought. However you do it, simply writing it down will probably prompt you to spend 10 to 20 percent less. I've yet to meet anyone who hasn't found at least one thing she's spending more on than she realized. If you stay unconscious about how you spend your money, you'll spend unknowingly, and your money will slip away. You'll never accomplish your goals without control of your spending.

If you already have a computer program for handling your finances, you can enter your expenditures there. That way you'll be able to really analyze every aspect of your spending. Microsoft Money and Quicken are two popular examples of this type of software. (More on this later in the chapter.)

Tracking your spending will also heighten your awareness of your buying patterns and make you think about the money you spend. For example, the next time you're in the grocery store checkout line and pick up a magazine, I hope you'll look at the price and think: *Do I really want to spend $5.95 on this magazine?* Whether or not you choose to buy the magazine is your decision. It's not about deprivation. It's about *awareness* and making conscious, informed choices.

Take the fourteen-day money-tracking challenge

If you're like me—and millions of other women—and you have difficulty sticking with your action steps, then I urge you to think of this pledge as a binding contract with yourself. It's an agreement to take an important step on your journey to financial fitness. If it helps, date and sign this contract.

It's a good idea to repeat this process at least twice a year until you think you have really mastered the art of spending wisely.

If this is a hot-button issue for you, you may want to track your spending for several months or until you feel more in control.

My pledge:

- I will track my spending for _____ days.
- I will write down everything I buy, including how much I spent and what I bought. This includes purchases made with cash, checks, debit cards, credit cards, and so on.
- I will carry a small notebook or empty checkbook register to record my purchases.

· PROFIT FROM HER STORY ·

Cassie says:
I was eating my money!

"I have made three significant changes to my financial well-being. I began using my online banking system's spending report function to track where I was spending the most money . . . of course it was in food. I noticed mainly that I was eating out quite a lot. I gave myself a weekly spending budget of $20, which could translate to up to three lunches if I were careful about my selections. I ordered my credit report and fixed an old medical bill that had been paid but not posted. I started calling around to get my auto loan refinanced and found another company that would offer me the same terms and drop my interest a whole five points! I also called my insurance agent and looked into life insurance for my husband and myself, and I'm planning to buy Microsoft Money or QuickBooks to start doing our financial statements."

DEVELOP A SPENDING PLAN

Did you notice I used the words *spending plan* instead of *budget*? The word *budget* reminds me of the word *diet*——and makes me think of shortage, self-denial, deprivation, and regret. Budget makes me think of things I want but can't afford. A spending plan puts *you* in control. It allows you to determine what's important to buy versus what you can buy just because it's there. I also recommend that you include your spouse/partner and children in the conversation about developing a spending plan. Many people ask me how their children can learn about money. I think your children's education starts at home. If you pay your kids an allowance, include it in your spending plan. Consider paying them their allowance by check and withholding for taxes so they get an idea of what will happen when they go to work and get a paycheck. You might also consider withholding for a 401(k) and investing their money.

> ### · PROFIT FROM HER STORY ·
>
> *Janice* says:
> Get your whole family involved!
>
> "I reviewed my spending and realized that a considerable amount of disposable income was disappearing at the grocery store. Our family devised a competition to see who could save the most money at the checkout stand for one week. Each person decided what the meals would be for the week and paid for the groceries with cash only ($150 total for the week). My daughter was the biggest saver!"

My friends give me a hard time, because when we're shopping together, I always review the items when I get to the sales counter. I look at each intended purchase and do my checkout checklist. I ask myself six important questions, and if the item passes the test, then I buy it. Okay, sometimes I keep the item, but often I decide not to buy it. However, it's always my choice. It reinforces that I control my money; it doesn't control me. You can print out a wallet-size version to remind yourself to review your choices before reaching for the cash or plastic. Here's my checkout checklist:

- Do I really want this?

- Do I need this?

- Will I use this?

- Am I buying this just because it's on sale?

- How many hours will I have to work to pay for this?

- Do I really love this?

· PROFIT FROM HER STORY ·

Wanda says:

It's the pause that refreshes your checkbook!

"I apply the twenty-four-hour rule to anything I want to buy that costs more than $25. The twenty-four-hour rule means whenever I see anything I want to buy that costs $25 or more, I go home, think about it, and wait twenty-four hours before buying the item. Most of the time I don't even remember what it was I wanted to buy. When I began tracking my spending, I found I was also dribbling away $30 a week on lattes. So I took that money and started an IRA, which I fund by having $50 automatically withdrawn from my checking account every month."

> **· PROFIT FROM HER STORY ·**
>
> *Beverly* says:
> Are you sure you're in love?
>
> "I talk to my friends about money quite a bit, because I see so many women who are slaves to their credit cards and jobs. I am always looking for information on this topic and eager to learn more so I can help myself and others. I went out today and returned some clothes that I did not absolutely love and saved $83! Then I went to Costco and spent $1.09 for a latte instead of the usual $2.70 plus a dollar tip."

If you've completed the fourteen-day challenge, congratulations! The next step is to summarize what you spent, using the monthly spending plan summary chart in the Appendix (you can also find it on the www.moneywisewomen.net website, under Financial Tips and Resources). If you want to start with how much you think you spend, fill in the projected expenses column, and then compare that to your actual spending at the end of the month. Add any of your own items that aren't listed.

So now what?

Here are some rough guidelines for how much of your income should be allocated to different expenses. You may need to make adjustments, depending on where you live. If you add or delete categories, you will need to revise the percentages.

- Housing and utilities: 30 percent
- Food: 15 percent
- Vehicles: 10 percent

- Insurance: 5 percent
- Savings and investing: 10 percent
- Childcare and education: 15 percent
- Entertainment: 5 percent
- Clothing: 5 percent
- Medical: 5 percent

Once you've personalized your categories and redistributed the percentages accordingly, you can look for ways to pare your expenses even further. For example, instead of using the full 5 percent on entertainment, revise the amount and redirect the money into another category. This would be a great way to increase the amount you contribute to savings and investing.

Are you overdrawn?

Use the information you've summarized to determine if you're spending responsibly (applause, applause!) and identify areas where you can trim your spending. It's your opportunity to analyze your spending, so you can determine what steps you need to take to control your outflow. I'll give you some ideas on how you can reduce your spending later in the chapter.

> · PROFIT FROM HER STORY ·
>
> *Kathleen* says:
> Every little bit does add up!
>
> "I paid my parents in full for a personal loan. This brings $100 a month back into my account. I also quit the long-distance phone

> service, which adds another $4 a month. Then I canceled our cable *TV Guide* for an additional $3.50 a month. I switched to a lower-cost but well-outfitted gym, saving me $20 a month. I'm also making larger payments on my aging car in hopes of paying it off within two years. And I'm filling out the necessary paperwork to increase my monthly contribution for my company retirement plan. I have written out on a huge piece of paper A PERSONAL PLAN FOR SUCCESS, which I'm hanging in my home office."

IT DOES COMPUTE

Several computer programs are available that make it easy to track your expenses and spending. Think of them as friendly bookkeepers who are always at your service. The two most common programs are Quicken and Microsoft Money. The programs can be used to keep your checkbook register, track business income and expenses, plan potential savings and budgets, track investments, track loans, and much more. Inputting the data from your personal checkbook register is a great way to review how you're spending your money. If you use online banking, some banks also now have a feature that allows you to categorize each expenditure in your checking account online, giving you another way to track your spending.

In a few clicks you can bake a colorful pie chart that shows how spending this month compares to other months or years. You can view year-to-date totals with subtotals of any or all spending categories. Let's say you're trying to save money by cutting back on grocery bills. A quick glance at a month-by-month comparison chart of that category shows how you're doing. Plus, once you customize that report, you can save it in favorites for quick use again.

If, like many people, you use the grocery store checkout as your "bank" and often take cash back when writing a check or using your debit card, be sure to log it into your program separately as cash and assign it to the appropriate spending categories. Otherwise your monthly grocery total may be incorrectly inflated, and you'll drive yourself nuts wondering how you spent $400 on Cheerios!

Another wonderful feature of this software is never having to do math in your checkbook. Both programs do the calculations for you. You still need to reconcile your register against your bank statement, but the computations to balance are minimal.

For business accounts, the convenience is priceless. You can set up your expense categories to match Schedule C (self-employment) deductions. At the end of each year, just print out summaries of income and expenses, and all the tedious work of tax preparation is done. You can even assign categories to match exact lines on tax forms. Plus it makes really neat, permanent records for the IRS. And again, no pesky math!

If your income is erratic, another useful feature is the monthly summary, which shows potential savings each month after expenses. It's a good nudge to transfer extra money to savings or an investment account.

Also, it's a breeze to set up automatic payments and deductions so you don't forget to record those. Microsoft Money even reminds you with a note at the bottom of the screen about upcoming payments. After you have entered payee names once, they will auto-fill from then on as you start to type the account name. It's a very intuitive program to learn and use, and most people will be able to jump right in with a very short learning curve, because it uses all the familiar Windows conventions. But help abounds within the program if you need it—there are even tutorial videos.

MEND AND TRIM YOUR SPENDING

The following is a long list I've developed of things you can do to revise your spending. I'm not suggesting you do everything on this list; just select several items that apply to you. The formula is simple: To get more money for something you really want, you need to spend less money on something else. It's like losing weight—eat less and exercise more. Tracking your spending will help you get more of what you want for your money—a bigger bang for your buck. Socrates had the right idea when he wrote: "Increase your income or decrease your wants."

- Before using your credit card to make a purchase, ask yourself: *Will this item be useable after I finish making payments?* If you pay your balance off monthly, this isn't an issue. But if you're charging your daily latte and you're not paying your credit card off monthly, that's a mighty expensive cup of coffee because you're also paying interest on the latte every month until your account is paid off. Other items in this category include dining out, movies, theater, and sporting events, just to name a few.

- I've noticed a potentially dangerous new trend here in the Pacific Northwest, and it's probably coming soon to a grocery store near you. My store is now offering a special credit card to buy groceries with that earns you rewards later on, such as free items. While this may seem appealing on the surface, it is rarely a good idea to buy consumable goods with a credit card. It usually signifies you are living beyond your means if you can't pay for your groceries by cash or check. Does it make sense to be paying for last year's Ben and Jerry's ice cream next year? Do you really want to be paying an extra 8 percent or 12 percent—or more—for orange juice and toilet paper? I didn't think so. Discover Card also fits into this category, with its cash-back reward based on how much you charge to the card. These plans are *only* for the very disciplined consumers who *always* pay off the card balances in *full* every month. Do not entertain this plan unless you are sure you fit into that category.

- Reacquaint yourself with beautiful, green cash and admire those handsome new Jacksons! When shopping, ask yourself: *Would I buy this item if I were paying cash?* Commit to not using your credit cards, checks, or debit card for one week. Pay cash for everything. You'll probably discover that it's much more difficult to spend cash than to use some form of paper or plastic. Try keeping a $100 bill in your wallet. It's much more difficult to spend a $100 bill than it is to fork over five $20s. I can tell you from personal experience that it's a lot harder to use cold, hard cash to buy something.

- Before buying, ask yourself: *How long will this be useful to me?* Think about it before you buy a video of a movie you may watch only a few times.

- Keep an I WANT list. We've become a nation devoted to instant gratification. We don't want to wait to buy anything. Make your wish list, plan your purchases, and then try waiting at least a week before buying something on your list. You may be surprised at how many things drop off your want list before you waste money on them! For things that remain on your list, try to be patient and watch for sales.

- Before you buy something, think about how many hours you had to work to pay for it. For example, if you're buying an $80 dress and you earn $14.55 an hour (after taxes are withheld), you worked five and one-half hours for the dress. Is it really worth that much of your effort?

- Set money limits before you go shopping. Determine how much you're going to spend before you head off to the mall. If you don't think you can stay within your limits, don't go, or take only cash. Leave your credit cards at home.

- Lock your credit cards in your safe deposit box, and simply don't use them except for true emergencies. Or, if you carry a credit card for emergencies, write EMERGENCY ONLY in red ink on a piece of paper and wrap it around the card. You'll think twice before using the credit card for nonemergencies.

- Never carry a credit card unless you plan to use it. An exception for recovered overspenders would be: My husband and I use our credit card to buy everything, because we get free airline miles with the card. However, we *always* pay our balance off monthly. Always.

- Avoid paying costly ATM fees by using only ATMs that don't have a usage fee; keep within your bank's network whenever possible, even if you have to go a little farther than is convenient, to avoid that extra charge.

- Keep a sharp eye on your checking account balance—those hefty overdraft fees are an awful waste.

- If you have a cell phone, watch your cell phone company's advertisements. If you see a lower rate, call the cell phone company and request the lower rate—it works!

- Check your telephone service and eliminate those add-on services, such as caller ID, call waiting, and call forwarding.

- Don't shop for celebration or recreation—find a less expensive hobby. Instead, plan your purchases and find other enriching ways to celebrate your successes and enjoy your downtime.

- Never shop for emotional comfort when you're upset or angry. Women are notorious for using retail therapy as an excuse to shop. We shop if we've had a bad day at work, or we've had a fight with our husbands or partners, or any number of other reasons. Find more sustaining ways to soothe and nurture yourself.

- Before you buy anything that costs more than $100, wait twenty-four hours. If you see something you really want and it costs more than $100, put it on hold. If you still want it the next day, go back and buy it. Most of the time, you'll forget what it was by the next day. I call this my "meant to be" theory. If you decide you want it and it's not there when you go back—it wasn't meant to be.

- Never pay retail prices. Sunny Kobe Cook, founder of Sleep Country USA, doesn't pay full price for any of her clothing. Instead she shops at TJ Maxx, Marshall's, Ross, and other discount stores. And, believe me—Sunny could easily afford to pay full price!

- Shop at local resale shops, discount centers, and factory outlets.

- Buy generic items in the grocery store.

- Plan menus before you go grocery shopping. Don't shop when you're hungry!

- Shop with a list, and stick to it!

· PROFIT FROM HER STORY ·

Debbie says:
We have made a dramatic change in
the amount we save each pay period!

"My husband and I have our paychecks deposited directly into our savings account instead of the checking account. We determine how much is needed for the monthly expenses and have that amount transferred into our checking account. This way, if we earn extra money on overtime, it stays in our savings account and doesn't disappear into the day-to-day spending."

- Don't make any impulse purchases. If you can't resist, keep the receipt, and don't use the item for at least a week. If you can live without it, take it back. Sometimes I buy something, get home, and realize I didn't really need it or love it. Because I keep my receipts, I can just take it back and get a refund.

- Don't buy something *just* because it's on sale. Everyone loves to get a bargain, but if you're not going to use it, don't buy it. This has been a really hard habit for me to break. Every time I find something on sale that I think I want to buy, I stop and ask myself: *Do I really need this, or am I buying it just because it's on sale?* Most of the time I don't buy it.

- Don't buy any new clothes until you have your present wardrobe paid for. If you don't pay your Nordstrom's account off every month, don't buy any more clothing until you've paid off the balance. Now, ladies, this can be a really tough one!

- Go through your closet before you go shopping for new clothes. Recently I found a pair of black pants tucked away in my closet with the receipt hanging on them. I was shocked, especially because I'm always talking about this stuff, but also because I couldn't remember when or where I bought them!

- Think twice before buying clothing that requires dry cleaning. It's amazing how expensive dry cleaning can be.

- Maintain your car properly so it will last longer. Changing the oil every three thousand to five thousand miles can save hundreds of dollars during the life of your car and help it live a longer life.

- Stop subscribing to magazines you don't read. Think about how many magazines you receive each month but never have time to read. Even if your subscription was a great deal, it's a waste of money if you're not reading the magazine. Share magazine subscriptions with your friends, or go to the library to read the magazine.

- Learn to love the sound of dropping your extra change into a jar every day. At the end of the month, use your cache of coins to open a contingency account for unexpected, irregular, or emergency expenses, and keep adding to it.

- If you get a raise, cost of living increase, or unexpected cash, celebrate it by saving it. The key to success with increases in income is to have the money automatically withdrawn from your payroll check or bank account and deposited into your savings account before you see it. Otherwise the temptation to spend it will be too great.

- Take your lunch to work, but treat yourself to eating lunch out once or twice a month so you don't feel deprived.

- Skip the daily latte and order drip coffee instead, or bring your coffee from home.

- Cut your cable television back to basic service.

- Don't buy videos—rent them instead. Unless you have children you probably won't watch the video more than a couple of times. Renting instead of buying will reduce your clutter and cost less. Subscribe to Netflix, Blockbuster, or other video service. They offer several monthly plans, which are often less than renting videos, and there's never a late fee! Or support your local video store if you're not susceptible to late returns. Another option is to check at your local library, because libraries often have good collections of videos and DVDs you can rent for free. Plus they'll happily order entire series of videos for you from regional libraries.

- Go to matinees instead of more expensive evening movies, and skip the nickel-a-kernel popcorn!

- Use long-distance calling cards—many of them are much less expensive than a monthly plan. I don't have long-distance service anymore. My long-distance calling card is less than $.03 a minute, including calls within the state. Another option is to use free Internet calling. (Visit www.skype.com for more information.)

- Stop buying lottery tickets.

- Make hair appointments every six weeks instead of every four weeks.

- Do your own manicures, or take turns with a friend; you do her manicure, and she does yours.

- Color your own hair and watch for sales on your brand.

- Watch for free events in your area. You might be delightfully surprised to find free concerts in the park, live music at local festivals, and much more.

- Stay clear of fast-food restaurants. Many people have asked me about the reason for this tip. I don't have children, but I know many women who do. They often zip through the fast-food drive-through lane to save time instead of preparing meals at home. These can be costly meals, depending on how often you go and how many people you're feeding. Plus they're rarely good for your health!

- Buy and assemble your meals from companies such as Dream Dinners. You'll save money by not buying groceries and then throwing them out because they've rotted; you'll also save time.

- Always turn off appliances that are not being used. Don't leave the television on if you're outside working in the yard.

- Run the dishwasher and washing machine only with full loads.

- Keep your thermostat at sixty-eight degrees or lower during the winter. Turn your heat off at night. Check with your local utility companies for other energy- and cost-saving ideas, including rebates for energy efficiency. One company here in Washington offers a 20 percent reduction in your monthly bill if you'll agree to some barely noticeable modifications to your heating and cooling. Now that's *cool!*

- Ask your utility company if it offers a budget payment plan. Although this doesn't trim any of your spending, it helps you with your monthly bill paying. This plan minimizes large fluctuations in energy bills from season to season because the utility company determines the monthly payment based on one-twelfth of the previous year's energy charges.

- Switch to taking digital photos, and never buy film or pay for processing again. You'll get better photos, because you'll actually take more when you aren't worrying about the cost of film. Delete the bad ones and archive the rest on CDs.

- Plan errands carefully to cover the least mileage.

- Examine your car insurance and home insurance deductibles. If you raise your deductibles, you can reduce your premiums. Determine how often you file claims. If you decide not to file a claim when you have a loss because you don't want it to affect your premiums, you may want to increase your deductibles. But make sure you have enough money set aside in case you have a loss. For example, if your deductible is $500, it's important to have $500 that is easily accessible in savings.

- Reduce your mortgage payments by refinancing. If you carry private mortgage insurance (PMI), make sure you really need it, or ask your lender to drop it. PMI is extra insurance lenders require from most home buyers who obtain loans for more than 80 percent of their home's value. In other words, buyers who put less than 20 percent down are normally required to pay PMI. If the value of your home has increased, you can probably get the PMI requirement waived.

- After a loan is repaid, make the payments to yourself instead of to the bank. You're already accustomed to the monthly payment. But divert the money to another account, because if you let the money go into your checking account, you'll spend it. Most of us just aren't that disciplined.

- Beware of online shopping! It's incredibly easy to go online and spend money. Follow the same guidelines listed earlier and, wield the same checkout checklist. A lot of deals can be found online, but if you can't be disciplined and resist excessive Internet shopping, and you have your credit card memorized, call your creditor(s) and ask them to give you a new credit card number. Put the card away, and don't memorize the number.

- If you do shop online, use price-comparison sites such as www.BizRate.com or www.PriceGrabber.com to find the best prices for things, especially major purchases. You may learn which store in your area has the best deal, or you may discover the item is cheaper online. Just be sure to add in the cost of shipping, if additional. When buying online, peruse the website for Internet-only specials. Plus you'll often save sales tax, unless the item is shipped from your state.

- Many online retailers have ongoing coupon promotions; always Google the store name before making your purchase final. For example, if you're about to buy printer cartridges from Staples, type this in at Google: STAPLES COUPONS. The search results should give you any currently available coupons, though it may take a bit of digging to find them. Or you could just search for coupons and visit one of the many all-coupon sites and browse by category. Just don't fall into the trap of buying something simply because you found a discount.

- Many companies have rewards programs that either give you cash back or reward you with something else of value, such as airline miles. I buy my office supplies and have all my workshop handouts photocopied at my local Office Depot using my rewards card, which provides me a quarterly reward check. I love receiving that check, which has been as much as $117. We also save lots of money using a local discount card, the Kitsap Card. Another discount card that's available throughout the United States is the Entertainment Card.

My husband and I also love our Alaska Airlines Visa card, because we earn mileage, which gives us free flights. We also get one $50 companion fare annually, so when we fly together, one of us pays the full fare, but the second person pays only $50. We charge everything we can (without a fee) on our card. This includes our insurance premiums and utilities (cable TV, phone, Internet service, newspaper, etc.). Words of caution: This is a good deal *only if you pay your balance off monthly.* If you carry a balance on your credit card, this isn't a good deal!

Fill in this pledge by selecting things from the list above or adding your own action steps.

I commit to the following action steps to reduce my spending:

_____
_____
_____
_____
_____
_____
_____
_____
_____
_____
_____
_____
_____
_____
_____
_____
_____

We tend to squander lots of money on gifts for others, especially during the holiday season. I think it's easier for us to justify spending money on someone else. Review your gift list to determine if you really need to give gifts to everyone on the list. Write a list of the people you plan to buy gifts for this year and stick to it! Make your gifts from the heart, because they mean more. Isn't that what gift giving is all about? Here are some low-cost, no-cost, or unique gift suggestions.

- Give a gift certificate for a day of chores, yard work, house cleaning, window washing, or car washing. This is a great idea for elderly parents and grandparents.

- Give a gift certificate to spend the day together doing something fun. Our parents and grandparents often appreciate the gift of time more than a store-bought gift. One Christmas my husband, Steve, gave me a handmade card that read: GOOD FOR ONE DAY TRIP TO THE COAST WITH STEVE AND OUR DOGS, SCRUFFY AND MISSY. When I asked him where he got the idea, he told me he read it in one of my newspaper columns!

- Cook a week's worth of dinners, freeze them, and deliver them to someone who's too busy or unable to cook.

- Involve the kids in baking holiday cookies and other delights. Take them along to deliver the goodies to an elderly neighbor and instill thrifty habits in the next generation.

- Consider a gift certificate for a massage, manicure, pedicure, and so on for mothers who often put their family's needs before their own.

- For children, buy a U.S. Savings Bond, open a mutual fund, or contribute to their future education through an Education Savings Account. Both parents and grandparents can buy any of the above.

- Offer to take a child to an art or science museum, and give Mom a break in the bargain.

- If you're crafty, consider making your gifts. People love things that have been personalized just for them.

- Give prepaid phone cards; they are a great gift for people who make lots of long-distance calls.

- Make handmade cards, including thank you, sympathy, get well, birthday, congratulations, and so on. This is a good project for parents and children to do together for grandparents. My mother loves receiving cards and telling her friends the cards were handmade by her daughter. Plus it's fun and good for your soul to express your creativity. (Just don't get seduced into buying $100 worth of art supplies to do it!)

- Write a letter to family members telling them how much you love and appreciate them. We live in a world where email has become the common way to communicate, but most people appreciate receiving handwritten letters in the mail.

- Make your own wrapping paper. Vegetable prints are fun for kids, or try stenciling. Cut open brown paper bags and try spray painting through pressed leaves.

- Buy movie gift certificates for people who enjoy films but can't afford the ticket price.

- Give a Netflix or Blockbuster subscription, or a local video store membership or gift certificate, to people who enjoy watching movies, documentaries, and TV shows. A subscription can be for one month, several months, or an entire year. You can make the first selection to get them started.

- Make a compilation video of the past year's family events for grandparents.

- Try a family white elephant gift exchange. My friend Nancy's family has a great time every Christmas with their gift exchange. Each family member buys a unisex gift. There's no price range, and gifts can be regifted—a silver basket showed up many years. Some people buy funny gifts; some people buy their gift at garage sales or the thrift store. The whole idea is to have fun with it. For the actual gift exchange, everyone draws a slip of paper with a number on it. Number one picks first. The second person can either steal number one's gift or unwrap another gift. After a gift has been stolen twice, it's frozen and can't be stolen again.

· PROFIT FROM HER STORY ·

Elyse says:
Make something they'll use every single day!

"For my father's eightieth birthday (which falls in December), I created a one-of-a-kind calendar keepsake. I went through all my family photos and scanned in about five or six for each month. Then, using my computer, I made a collage that was relevant to each month. For example, July featured images from various Fourth of July celebrations through the years. January recalled a ski vacation from thirty years earlier. September showed off back-to-school photos from my grade school years. The result was a family history in photos. At most office supply stores you can buy calendar kits that have the paper and templates all prepared, and then you just print it on your color printer. It's something to be enjoyed every day for a year and then saved as a wonderful remembrance. And the cost was under $20!"

- Donate to a charitable organization. I buy several fresh wreaths from Hospice of Kitsap County to send to relatives and friends who don't live in the area. It supports a wonderful organization, 50 percent of the purchase price is tax deductible (if you itemize your deductions), and the wreath is great way to share the Pacific Northwest with others. My sister-in-law makes donations to a needy family in our name. It's kind of a two-for-one gift.

- Make photo books of the kids, which are treasured by parents and grandparents. If you have a computer, it's easy to add fun captions and so on to digital photos. Photo shops sell small, inexpensive bound books to preserve your pictures.

- Personalize accessories with a photo. Most photo shops and many other gift shops now offer all sorts of inexpensive personalization services. Just take in a favorite photo, and you can have it applied to a mug, mouse pad, key chain, T-shirt—you name it! Many online services offer the convenience of storing your digital photos, along with all these customizable options right at your fingertips.

As you can see by now, you have many, many ways to reduce your spending without making huge sacrifices. Just pick a few to begin with that feel right for you. Who says it can't be fun? Make a game out of it, and challenge yourself to find ways to pinch every last drop out of your pennies. The whole point of spending less is to be able to save more.

Next on the list is cleaning out the basement of your financial house and taming the monster down there that no one wants to talk about.

· FIVE ·

Get Out of Credit Card Debt

How to evaluate and eliminate debts that are
undermining the foundation of your financial house

Chapter Goals for You

- Take the debt quiz to see where you stand, sit, or limp

- Determine your total debt

- Study the debt reduction ideas and choose some to pursue

- Read *all* the fine print on *all* your credit accounts and be sure you understand all the potential hidden fees

- Store your credit cards where they are not easy to get

- Decide if transferring balances is right for you

- Create a debt-reduction plan and timeline

- Use an online debt-reduction planner and calculator

I f you have no credit card debt or never use credit cards, give yourself a hearty round of applause. Heck, do a few cartwheels if you can! However, you might still want to read this chapter to ward off any future temptations to debt. Or perhaps you'll decide to share it with others who do have this challenge.

THE TRUTH OF PAINFUL CONSEQUENCES

If your financial house is built on rotting timbers, they have to go. And those dangerous floorboards are the debt that jeopardizes all your financial plans. (I'm talking about debt accrued from both general-purpose credit cards such as Visa or American Express and from revolving accounts you may have with department or specialty stores or with gasoline companies.) Debt can prevent you from getting the car or house of your dreams—or at the very least, propel you into a high interest rate. A friend with spotty credit who hadn't owned a car in a few years was aghast when she realized the only car loan she could get was at 49 percent interest! And that was for a car with more than two hundred thousand miles on it.

If you haven't yet experienced real-world consequences for racking up big credit card debt, trust me—those nasty consequences are lurking behind your next credit application or credit check like termites in your two-by-fours. Say you want to move to a nicer apartment in a new building. Don't be surprised if a credit check is required and if the results prohibit you from moving in. And did you know insurance companies also check your credit before deciding what rate to offer you?

Debt can undermine nearly every financial transaction you hope to make one day—and even affect other aspects of your life. Savvy singles are now seeking financial advice—and credit checks—before they walk down an aisle to money misery. Even certain kinds of jobs require a background—and credit—check to evaluate your character.

So if you needed more reasons to demolish your debt, there they are.

There's such a thing as good debt

Good debt is anything that has the potential to increase in value. Your home mortgage is good debt, because property usually increases in value. Another example of good debt is a student loan, since college graduates generally earn more than nongraduates, so it makes good sense as an investment in yourself.

According to financial expert Suze Orman, bad debt sacrifices tomorrow's needs for today's desires. Another well-known financial author, David Bach, says if debt doesn't have potential to increase in value, then it's bad debt. The bottom line: Bad debt is credit card debt, department store debt, automobile loans, and any other debt you owe for things that don't gain value.

And there's an exception—if you're very disciplined!

As mentioned earlier, this advice applies *only* if you are disciplined enough to pay off your credit card bill in *full* every month. If you are paying cash, debit, writing checks, or using a card with no points/premiums or benefit to you—*why???* All those methods benefit the bank or the business—not you. You can earn all sorts of valuable rewards by putting as many of your purchases as possible on credit cards. If you would rather accumulate points toward a car, or fan points for sports tickets, fine. Get a card with those types of rewards; just make sure you are getting something for the business you do, and then charge everything. But don't get caught by surprise with a bill you can't pay off in full. Write down every credit card purchase in your checkbook register along with any checks or debits. This will ensure you have the month to pay your credit card bill when it arrives, and you'll be earning mileage or other rewards at the same time.

> ### · PROFIT FROM HER STORY ·
> #### *Carol* says:
> #### Paying the tuition bill is a little less painful now!
>
> "I'm slowly plugging away at my action steps. Sometimes I take a few steps backward, which seems to cancel out my forward movement. That said, I feel fortunate to be more coherent about how I spend my money. In the past eight months, I obtained the services of a financial planner for the first time in my life, and I also refinanced my mortgage (including consolidating debt). I got an Alaska Airlines Visa card, which I don't think I could have gotten before reining in some of my debt. It's great, because now I charge my son's college tuition and also earn rewards mileage—but I have followed your warning, and I always pay off the balance in full every month. I got my first IRA and recently bought a CD that yields way more than the cheesy savings account I've been putting money into for the past several months. Next, I'm going to significantly increase my Thrift Savings Plan, 401(k) contribution, and change my withholdings to keep more money in my pockets instead of Uncle Sam's. I really am starting to feel wise about money!"

THE ELEPHANT IN THE BASEMENT

Isn't it interesting that in our society we are willing to talk about relationships, problems with our children and parents, trouble at work, and so on, but we won't discuss debt? Would you tell your best friend that you owe $10,000 in credit card debt? Most of us wouldn't share this information, and it often results in low self-esteem, depression, anxiety, and relationship problems.

According to Bankrate.com, the average credit card debt per household in the United States is approximately $14,500, and the typical American family pays about $1,200 a year in credit card interest. Think about this, and take time to let it sink in. We're not talking about credit card purchases; we're talking about *interest* on these purchases. When you pay interest, you are literally paying for *nothing*. Imagine—taking a $100 bill, tearing it to pieces, and throwing it away. That's what you're doing when you are paying interest. You're throwing your hard-earned money away.

When I started reading grim statistics such as that back in 1996, it really struck a chord. I realized it was time to develop a plan to pay off our very high credit card balance. I'm sharing this with you because I don't want you to think that you're alone. Since I started Money Wi$e Women, many people have confided to me that they lug around credit card debt ranging from $10,000 to $50,000. And many are self-employed women who financed their businesses using their credit cards. It often plunges them into a deep financial hole when they are just starting to make money. Anyone who's ever been mired in credit card debt knows it's not easy to dig yourself out. But if you're determined and committed, it can be done.

Get started by taking the following quiz.

Debt quiz

Go ahead and write in the answers. You'll enjoy reading them later when you can give different replies.

1. Do you seem to worry about money most of the time?
   O YES   O NO

2. Has living paycheck-to-paycheck become a normal routine for you?
   O YES   O NO

3. Do you use credit card cash advances to pay your bills?
   O YES   O NO

4. Do you pay only the minimum payment due on your credit cards?
   O YES   O NO

5. Are you near or at the credit limits on your credit cards?
   O YES   O NO

6. Are you concerned you'll receive calls from your creditors, or have you already had accounts turned over to collection agencies?
   O YES   O NO

7. Do you find you sometimes have to borrow money from friends or family to pay your bills?
   O YES   O NO

8. Have you ever thought about or filed for bankruptcy?
   O YES   O NO

9. Each month do you charge more on your account than you make in payments?
   O YES   O NO

10. Are you worried that your spending habits are jeopardizing your future?
    O YES   O NO

11. Does it feel as if you're always late paying your bills?
    O YES   O NO

12. Do you feel you need to earn more money to keep up?
    O YES   O NO

How much do you owe?

If you answered yes to any of these questions, it's time to take the next step, which is admitting you're in credit card debt. If you're ready to be debt free, begin by summarizing your credit card debt using the following credit card summary chart.

List your debts in order, starting with the highest interest rate, and be sure to date your list.

CREDIT CARD	CURRENT BALANCE	INTEREST RATE	MINIMUM MONTHLY PAYMENT
	$	%	$
	$	%	$
	$	%	$
	$	%	$
	$	%	$
	$	%	$
	$	%	$
	$	%	$
	$	%	$
TOTAL	$	%	$

· PROFIT FROM HER STORY ·

Lori says:

Ignoring your debt doesn't make it go away!

"One of the most difficult things for me to come to grips with about my life thus far is that I managed to rack up a considerable amount of credit card debt without knowing exactly how it happened. Somehow it sneaked up on me through the years. I was always robbing Peter to pay Paul. Between raising my boys, handling my medical bills, and loss of work time, I was a financial wreck. I spent many years refusing to face it. I couldn't bear to add it all up, so I really didn't know how much my total debt was. In some strange way I thought that maybe ignoring it would make it go away! I even went through periods of unnecessary charging on my cards—buying clothes and so on to make myself feel better! The reality was that it was a huge weight on my shoulders that I had been carrying alone for most of my adult life.

▶

"Shortly after our whirlwind romance began, Mark accepted a job out of the country. We began to plan our lives together. The problem was that I could not bring myself to tell him about my financial situation. He was only one year out of a marriage that cost him most of his savings. As the months passed by, we were making plans for me to move out of the country to join him, and I was being eaten up inside trying to figure out what to do. I either had to fess up about the nightmare I was going through or figure out a way to sufficiently hide it.

"I finally decided to add up all the bills: a whopping $50,000!!! Wow. I was in a much bigger mess than I had imagined. My first thought was that I somehow *had* to hide this ugly secret. But how? How was I going to go into a lasting relationship with something so big hanging over me? I immediately approached a consumer credit counseling agency to consolidate my debts. It took all the information, and I was given a figure of $1,250 per month for five years to get me out of debt. Wow again! Even with the negotiated interest rate, that was $75,000. How on earth was I going to hide that fact from my new significant other?

"Worse yet, I was struggling with the fact that I was going into a committed relationship with so much baggage attached. I felt guilty that I wasn't being forthcoming with the information, but I was petrified that he would run the other way.

"The other option that I began to entertain was to file bankruptcy. Now that I had an actual figure and realized just how bad it was, it was beginning to seem completely out of reach for me to be able to get out from under the debt. It was such a wonderful thought to wipe the slate clean and start my new life fresh and unencumbered. However, on the other hand, I was feeling tremendous guilt and shame over the fact that those bills were my responsibility. But after consulting an attorney I knew that bankruptcy was not an option I wanted to pursue.

> ▶
>
> "Ultimately Mark learned of my problems and showed that he still loved me after all! We had some lengthy discussions, but we have tackled the problem together. We have a plan to pay off my debt. I know it's going to take several years, but what a relief to know it's being handled. I now know that my debts do not define me as a person. I feel so much more in control of my life now. However, I learned that honest understanding is the only way I could start to solve my debt problem, and that denial is not the answer!"

The real cost of credit

Credit cards are expensive because the interest rates companies charge are almost always in the double digits. For example, if you have a credit card balance of $14,500 with an interest rate of 12.9 percent, and you are paying the minimum 2 percent payment each month, it will take you thirty-six years to pay off the balance. You will have paid $16,491 in interest and a total of $30,991. And, that's only *if* you don't use the card again! So whatever you were buying on sale wasn't really a good deal after all.

My first step in eliminating our $10,000 credit card debt was calling our credit card company to request a lower interest rate, and it worked! Next, we paid *more* than our minimum payment and funneled any extra money we received toward the credit card. It took a couple of years to pay our credit card off, but what a great feeling to reclaim our financial future!

You too can reclaim your financial freedom by developing an action plan to pay off your credit card debt. However, to succeed you must have a realistic spending plan (see Chapter Four), which helps you calculate how much money you have left each month for your credit card repayment plan, and where you can find more.

· PROFIT FROM HER STORY ·

Sunny Kobe Cook says:
Getting into debt is easier than getting out!

"I began my business career as a secretary in my hometown of Kansas City. When the cold and snow finally got to me, I applied for and received a transfer to my employer's Dallas, Texas office. Although I had a job waiting for me and warm, sunny weather, there was no salary increase. There's a big difference in the cost of living between Kansas City and Dallas. In Kansas City I paid $167.50 per month for my half of a two-bedroom house with a garage. In Dallas my rent was $495 per month for a tiny one-bedroom apartment. This was only one of the many sizable differences, and my secretarial salary didn't go nearly as far in 'Big D.'

"Without even realizing it, I began living on my credit cards. Just to maintain my normal standard of living, I got myself into credit card debt. In my moment of panic and looming financial crisis, I turned to my older sister. She asked me the most important question I've ever been asked, "So what are you going to do about it?" Put on the spot, I told her I thought I would have to get a part-time job. We did some brainstorming about the various part-time options available and concluded that a neighborhood furniture store was my best solution.

"For the next eighteen months, I worked every night, every weekend, and every holiday—thirty-two hours a week on top of my forty-hour weekday job. During that time I learned many very valuable things—I loved retail sales and home furnishings. I learned what customers wanted, what motivated sales staff, even which computer system worked best in this sort of setting. I made friends with all the manufacturers' representatives. Perhaps the most important thing I learned was about myself—I learned I actually *can* work that many hours!

▶

> "While working my part-time job, an idea began to take root—I could open my own furniture store. The economics of such a proposition ultimately changed the vision to a mattress store, the first of which opened in January 1991. With a $5,000 investment and the great relationships I had formed while working part time, I founded Sleep Country USA. Nine years later, in February 2000, when I sold my company, I had twenty-eight stores throughout a two-state area and a Canadian licensee with more than eighty stores in Canada."

TAKE THESE NEXT STEPS

The most important step in eliminating credit card debt is to quit using your credit cards. Period. Let's review one of my tips from Chapter Four: Lock your credit cards in your safe deposit box and simply don't use them except for true emergencies. Or, if you carry a credit card for emergencies, write EMERGENCY ONLY in red ink on a piece of paper and wrap it around the card. You'll think twice before using the credit card for nonemergencies purposes. Another option is to put your credit cards in a tin can, fill it with water, and freeze it. Why? Because you can't microwave a tin can!

A new pair of shoes is not an emergency, no matter how cute or how great the sale price.

According to Mikelann Valterra, financial counselor and author of *Why Women Earn Less: How to Make What You're Really Worth*:

> *You simply cannot get out of debt without saving money. The number one mistake people make when it comes to getting out of debt is they don't save money each month for periodic expenses. This is what keeps people locked in the debt cycle. Because debt is so*

stressful, people will often throw money at their debt as soon as they have any extra money. They don't put money into savings. But the problem is that life keeps happening. So there you are, trying hard to pay off your credit cards, when your car breaks down. Without having any savings, you use your credit cards again to fix the car, and your overall debt goes back up. The key is to save money each month for all those expected and unexpected sporadic expenses. It is better to pay your debt off slower and save money each month, than focus singlemindedly on your debt and not save money. This is short-term thinking. It may work for a while, but eventually something will happen, and you will incur more debt while you deal with the new expense. If you save money each month, you will have the money to prevent new debt while you continue paying off the old debt.

If you must continue to use your credit cards, deduct the amount of each purchase in your checkbook register. This ensures you will have the money to pay the full amount charged when your bills arrive.

Next, call your creditors to request a lower interest rate. It's best to call early in the day in the middle of the week, because there are fewer people calling. Make sure you've got a smile on your face, and be polite. Your end of the conversation might go something like this: "I'm calling to request a lower interest rate on my credit card. I receive lower interest rate offers from other companies every day. I don't really want to change companies, but it's not wise for me to continue paying this rate. Can you offer me a similar interest rate?"

Most of the time the customer service representative will put you on hold while he or she reviews your record. If you've been making your payments on time, and you're a long-time customer, you have an excellent chance of getting a lower interest rate. If the representative comes back and tells you that the company is unable to offer you a lower interest rate, take it one step further. Explain that you've had a credit card with the company for x number of years and really don't want to take your business elsewhere. Ask the representative, "Are you sure this is the lowest interest rate you can offer me?"

If the representative doesn't reduce the interest rate, ask to speak to a supervisor. Once the supervisor gets on the line, repeat the conversation you had with the customer service representative, including how long you've been a customer and that you don't really want to take your business elsewhere, but it's not in your best interest to keep it with this company at the higher interest rate.

A couple of online resources will help you find good interest rates—www.bankrate.com and www.cardratings.com.

When you set up your debt reduction plan, I recommend you begin by paying extra money on the credit card with the lowest balance. Some experts recommend you start by paying off the credit card with the highest interest rate, and if you are disciplined and know you will stick to your plan, go ahead and do that. But I think you'll have a better chance of success if you pay the credit card with the lowest balance first. Why? Because when it's paid off, you'll feel a sense of accomplishment. It's like losing weight. If you think about the long-term goal, you might get discouraged. Taking small steps will help ensure your success.

Next, pay off the credit card with the highest interest rate. As you pay off one account, increase the amount you pay on your other accounts, thus accelerating the payments. If you're unable to control your credit card spending, close your accounts as you pay them off. When you close it, ask the creditor to annotate that the account was CLOSED AT CONSUMER'S REQUEST. This is important, because closing accounts shows up on your credit report and could adversely affect your credit score. *Don't close the account that you've had the longest, because this might reduce your credit score.* (More on this in Chapter Six.)

Continue paying off accounts with the highest interest rate first. This may feel like the toughest challenge you've ever faced, especially if you're a newly reformed recreational shopper. But read on, as there are some ways to make it less painful. Most important is to keep your debt-free goals clearly in view. And take heart from the stories of women who've been there and done it.

> ### · PROFIT FROM HER STORY ·
> *Linda* says:
> Consolidation may help!
>
> "I went ahead with the debt consolidation yesterday. The company told me that it goes on your credit report only if you negotiate a settlement, which I'm not doing. I consolidated it with a company that makes the payments for me, and it can get an automatic rate reduction in interest—a couple of my cards were over 20 percent!!! I checked the company out with the Better Business Bureau, and it seems to be legitimate. All I know is that I feel as if a big weight has been lifted off me!"

More debt reduction tricks

Let's talk about some additional steps you can take to ensure your credit card reduction plan is successful. If your credit card has an annual fee, request the fee be removed. If you have trouble making your credit card payments on time because the due date falls before your paycheck, call your credit card company to request a billing date that better suits your needs. When my husband and I began receiving our pension checks on the first of the month, I struggled to make our credit card payment on time, because the payment date came before our checks arrived. I called my credit card company, requested a later billing date, and my request was approved. It removed the stress of worrying every month how we were going to pay the bill on time. I've also called my credit card company to get a different due date when I knew we were going to be on vacation when the bill came due. And it readily agrees to change the date.

· PROFIT FROM HER STORY ·

Marilyn says:
Save for your kids too!

"It feels sooooo good to be working my way out of debt and not wanting to go back into it. Wow! It feels good to be able to invest $200 a month in an IRA and $75 a month for Mimi. I've told several groups of women that I'm making my daughter's 50th birthday present now by investing $75 a month, and they can't believe they didn't think of doing that. So, it's fun to plant seeds for others too. I paid off $4,000 on my Visa and dropped the ceiling to $2,500, and I have $2,500 now in business savings. Life is good!"

Avoid hidden fees

Credit card companies are not only making a killing on the interest from unpaid balances, but also from various fees. They make money by charging high late fees and decreasing the grace period (the time between the date the statement is mailed and the date the payment is due). Most credit card companies will waive the late fee *one time* if you accidentally make a late payment.

Several years ago I didn't allow enough mail time for my credit card payment due January 1. Since the due date was a holiday and on a Sunday, I assumed the payment wouldn't be considered late until Monday, January 2. When I received my next credit card statement and discovered a sizable late fee along with interest on the charges, I realized I was wrong. I immediately called the credit card company to request the fee be waived, which it did, because I'd never had a late payment. Now I'm careful to allow plenty of time for my payment to arrive before the due date. Other alternatives to ensuring your payment arrives on time are to set up online bill paying or take your payment directly to the bank.

Always carefully review your credit card statements. My credit card company has made the same mistake on a bill twice in a six-month period. I charge everything and pay the entire bill off every month. One month I wrote a check for $2,560, and the credit card company credited my account for $25.60, which means I paid interest on the unpaid balance. I resolved the error, and the interest was credited to my account, but had I not carefully reviewed my statement, I probably would have missed it.

Beware of making late payments, because most credit card company terms include a clause to increase the interest rate if you make even one late payment. (Some loan companies also do this, so check all your finance contracts for this painful catch.) Under the Universal Default Policy, credit card companies can automatically increase their customers' interest rate—sometimes as high as 25 percent to 30 percent—for missing a payment, even if the payment is missed on a *different* credit card issued by a different company! If you have never missed a payment on a particular credit card, you can still be penalized for being late on a different credit card. Bottom line: *Read the fine print!!!*

Credit card companies used to increase your credit limit whenever you exceeded the limit. Now they're charging fees for cardholders who exceed their limits by as little as $1. Credit card companies also charge fees for cash advances. In addition, cash advances usually cost you a higher interest rate than purchases, which aren't lowered until you've completely paid off your balance. Always read the fine print to determine the applicable fees *before* you take a cash advance.

· PROFIT FROM HER STORY ·

Mary says:
I found a creative way to pay off my credit cards!

"I implemented some of the key steps I learned for getting myself out of debt. I'm a single mother of four, divorced two years ago, and was struggling to get control of my financial situation. I had just started a job that was finally paying what I needed to get by, but I had two years of 'catch up' on my debt. I started by reorganizing my debt by refinancing my home, which paid off roughly 45 percent of my credit card debt. Then I used my tax return to pay off another 35 percent of my credit card debt. I've taken my credit cards and put them in my sock drawer; they are there for emergencies but are no longer an easy temptation when I'm at the mall or if I'm feeling too lazy to go into the gas station and pay for my fuel. I buy only things for myself that I *love*, not just like. I refuse to buy something simply because it's a good deal, even 75 percent off. I feel incredibly empowered by taking these steps. I am in control of my finances now, and I see a light at the end of the tunnel."

Beware of balance transfers

I'm often asked if it's a good idea to transfer credit card balances to a new company advertising a lower interest rate if you transfer your current balance. My advice: Be cautious and *read the fine print*. The lower interest rate may apply for only a short time and then jump to a rate as high or higher than what you previously had. If you don't qualify for the advertised premium card interest rate, some companies substitute a lower-grade card, which means you could end up paying a higher interest rate than before you transferred. Opening new credit card accounts can also have an adverse effect on your credit score, which I'll discuss in the next chapter.

One option is to transfer balances on your cards with higher interest rates to your accounts with lower interest rates. If your credit cards are maxed out, call your credit card companies with lower interest rates to ask if they can increase your limit. Explain you're planning to transfer balances from higher-rate accounts. And don't forget that you can ask your credit card company to reduce your interest rate.

Be proactive

If you're having trouble making ends meet, contact your creditors immediately. Don't wait for them to start writing and/or calling you. Explain your circumstances, and try to negotiate a modified payment plan to reduce your monthly payments to a manageable level.

· PROFIT FROM HER STORY ·

Theresa says: Why I love my debit card!

"I have to write only one check a month now, and that too will soon end. I pay most of my bills by automatic deduction from my checking account, and for everything else, I use my debit (ATM) card. I find it super convenient, and I never have to worry about having enough cash with me. If I need it, I can also get cash with my card at ATMs, banks, grocery stores, and many other kinds of stores. It is accepted just about everywhere and is much faster than writing a check. Even the post office accepts it and offers cash back. And though my bank statement shows a list of those expenditures each month, I always make sure I enter debit purchases in my check register as soon as I get home. That way, there are no nasty surprises on the statement! And best of all, it relieves me of the need to have a major credit card, because I can use it just like a Visa card to buy things online, reserve cars and hotels, and so on—with one important catch. The full amount of the purchase must already be in the account the card is attached to. Which is exactly what I like it about it—it prevents me from spending money I don't have, and as a result, I have zero credit card debt. You'd be surprised how much stuff you can live very well without if you know you are spending real money in real time!

"The only downside (and this also goes for credit cards) is it's possible to have your account compromised if someone gets hold of your account number and expiration date. This happened to me last year. I'm thankful my bank (Washington Mutual) monitors all debit and credit purchases for unusual activity and calls customers the minute it spots something. My bank simply closed my card, sent me a new card, and credited my account with the amount taken. And despite that inconvenience, I was not deterred from using my card almost daily."

CHANGE FOR THE BETTER

Read through the list below, fill in the blanks on the action steps you plan to take, and note your anticipated completion date.

To get out of credit card debt, I pledge to:

- Stop using my credit cards. ____/____/____
- Summarize my credit card debt using the credit card summary chart. ____/____/____
- Call my credit card companies to request a lower interest rate. ____/____/____
- Ask my creditor(s) to waive the annual fee. ____/____/____
- Consider transferring balances from accounts with higher interest rates to my accounts with lower interest rates. ____/____/____
- Start by paying off the credit card with the lowest balance. ____/____/____
- Pay more than the minimum monthly payment. ____/____/____
- Pay on time to ensure I don't have an additional late fee. ____/____/____
- As I pay off one account, increase the amount I'm paying on my other accounts, thus accelerating payments. ____/____/____
- Close the credit cards after they are paid off and request that my credit report indicate that the account(s) were closed at the consumer's request. ____/____/____
- Use the online debt reduction planner and calculator at www.fool.com to determine how long it will take to pay off each account at a particular interest rate and payment amount. ____/____/____

I hope by now that you can see a path out of the dark woods of debt. Remember, lots of other women have walked that same path and emerged with improved self-esteem and greater confidence in their ability to manage their money. And so can you!

Next we'll delve into a critical yet little understood facet of your personal finances. It may sound scary, or perhaps dull, but you must face up to your credit report and credit score.

SIX

Get Clear about Your Credit and Clear It Up!

How to decipher and repair your credit reports and credit score

---

Chapter Goals for You

- Order your credit reports
- Repair any errors
- Resolve any unpaid bills or collections
- Write any needed letters to dispute contested inaccuracies
- Check—and understand—your credit score
- Take steps to raise your credit score

HAVE YOU BEEN NAUGHTY OR NICE?

If someone looked in the windows of your financial house, what would she see? Would your house be neat and orderly, or would there be stacks of unpaid bills and unopened mail all over the place? In a way, that's what a credit report does. Your credit report is like an appraisal of your financial house—it's your credit profile. Some people are afraid to get their credit reports because they're afraid of what they'll find, but perhaps Alice can convince you.

· PROFIT FROM HER STORY ·

Alice says:
Just do it!

"I was fifty-six when I saw my first credit report—and it was as upsetting as I thought it would be. Yet I'm glad I got it, so I can start to correct it and deal with my credit problems. I always saw the credit agencies as the enemy (and still do, I suppose), as people who have too much control over my financial options with too little input from me. I figured the less they knew about me the better, which is one reason I never wanted to get my report—I knew I'd have to give them information first. I still hate the impersonal nature of banks and credit companies and wish there were a way to have a more authentic relationship with people about money. Anyway, scrutinizing the reports has to be done if you are in a position to need credit from anyone for anything. Otherwise, you may end up paying a higher interest rate than you need to. So if you're in my leaky credit boat, order your free report and start patching!"

Exactly what's in this thing?

Your credit report contains information on where you work and live, the credit accounts that have been opened in your name, how you pay your bills, and whether you've been sued, arrested, or filed for bankruptcy. Checking your report regularly can help you catch mistakes and fraud before they play havoc with your personal finances. I recommend you request and review your credit reports at least annually.

I know it's not romantic, but if you're planning to get married, it's a good idea for you to sit down together and review your credit reports before your wedding date. It's extremely important to understand where each of you stands financially before you combine your assets. Once you are married, your credit will be blended. And since opposites often do attract, it's better to be prepared now than sorry later.

It's also important to review each other's credit reports if you're getting separated or divorced, because that same blended credit can easily harm or even destroy your credit profile. If you live in a community property state, you may be responsible for any debt your husband incurred during your marriage. You and your husband are both responsible for paying debt on joint accounts. If your divorce decree states that your husband is responsible for paying off certain accounts, but if he does not pay or does not pay on time, your creditors can hold you accountable. They don't care what the divorce decree says.

The best course of action on joint credit cards is to close the account. If there's a balance on the account, it cannot be closed, but you can request it be placed in inactive status and closed when it's paid in full.

The three doors

The three major credit-reporting agencies are Experian, Equifax, and TransUnion. You really do need to know what's behind all three doors. Request and review your credit report annually from *all three* credit-reporting agencies. Why? Because each one has a different database and could very easily contain different information—and different mistakes!

Equifax—www.equifax.com
(800) 685-1111

Experian—www.experian.com
(888) 397-3742

TransUnion—www.transunion.com
(877) 322-8228

Another reason to request and review your credit report(s) regularly is to monitor your credit report for identity theft. Identity theft is when someone uses your personal information in order to open accounts, obtain loans, and buy cars and other items without your permission. Chapter Seven will teach you how to protect yourself from identity theft.

You can now obtain your credit report *free* once every twelve months. Request your free credit report(s) online at www .annualcreditreport.com or by calling (877) 322-8228. The free credit reports are available only at the above website. If you order directly from any of the individual credit-reporting agencies, you'll be charged a fee. You can request your free credit report from each of the three credit-reporting agencies all at once. You can also spread out your monitoring by requesting your credit report from one credit-reporting agency, wait four months to request another credit report from a different credit-reporting agency, and request the last credit report four months later. If you want to obtain more than one credit report annually from the credit-reporting agencies, you'll have to pay a small fee.

The information you'll need to provide to receive a free copy of your credit report includes: your name, date of birth, Social Security number, current address, and previous address (if you lived there less than two years).

State law provides for the citizens of Colorado, Georgia, Maine, Maryland, Massachusetts, New Jersey, and Vermont to have free access to their credit reports. You can also receive a free credit report in a couple of other ways. If you've been denied credit, insurance, or employment because of the information supplied by a credit-reporting agency, contact the credit-reporting agency within sixty days of receiving a denial notice for a free report. You're also eligible for free credit reports if you certify in writing that:

- you're unemployed and plan to look for a job within sixty days, or

- you're on welfare, or

- your report is inaccurate because of fraud.

Your credit report is your credit profile. It provides a snapshot of how much you owe, how you pay your bills, whether you pay them on time, and other personal information about you. It's as important as the SATs are to college-bound high school students. Your credit score is your credit rating. Sometimes it is referred to as your FICO score. FICO stands for Fair Isaac Corporation, which developed the most commonly used model to calculate a credit score. Your credit score or FICO score is an assigned number, which is determined by the information in your credit report. The higher your number, the less risk you represent, and the better for you!

HOW TO SPOT SIGNS OF TROUBLE

When creditors review your credit report, they are looking for indicators of trouble, which may include:

- Total balances on your accounts are high in relationship to your income.

- You have too many accounts with balances owed. If you owe money to a large number of accounts, it might indicate that you're overextended.

- A high percentage of your total credit line is being used. If your credit cards are close to being maxed out, it suggests you might have trouble making your payments in the future.

- You are continually making minimum and/or late payments, which can have a huge negative impact.

- There have been too many inquiries in the past twelve months. I'll discuss inquiries later in the chapter.

- You have opened too many accounts in the past twelve months.

- Bad debts have been turned over to collection agencies.

The list above contains some of the things creditors are looking at when they review your credit report, but it's not an exhaustive list. Check out these resources to learn more:

The Motley Fool—www.fool.com

Federal Trade Commission—www.ftc.gov

Federal Citizen Information Center—www.pueblo.gsa.gov or (888) 878-3256

Fair Isaac Corporation—www.myfico.com

· PROFIT FROM HER STORY ·

Leta says:

Don't give your money away in interest payments!

"I pulled my credit reports, which aren't terribly bad, but I realized how many credit accounts I have opened (and closed) through the years, and I will *not* be doing that any longer. I expect I could have bought and sold a house or two with the interest I have been and still am paying!"

Verify the facts

When you're reviewing your credit report(s), make sure your personal information (name, date of birth, address, and employer) is accurate. Review all the accounts listed to ensure they belong to you. Carefully review each account—especially if you're divorced, separated from your spouse, or in the process of getting divorced—to ensure that all joint accounts have been closed and that any individual accounts that list either of you as an authorized user are closed. To close joint accounts, write a letter to the credit card company and request a final statement. If you're unable to pay off the balance, request that the account be placed in inactive status and closed once it's paid off. If your divorce decree shows your husband is responsible for paying a joint account and does not pay it, the credit card company will hold you responsible, and it will reflect negatively on both your credit reports. For more information on divorce and credit, visit the Women's Institute for a Secure Retirement at www.wiser.heinz.org. If someone else's name is listed on your account(s), your credit could be adversely affected. This includes cosigning for loans. My advice is to think twice before cosigning! For more information on individual and joint accounts, go back to Chapter Five.

> ### · PROFIT FROM HER STORY ·
>
> *Elaine* says:
>
> When you get divorced, sever every single financial partnership!
>
> One of my friends, Elaine, learned the hard way why this is important. Elaine has been married and divorced twice in the past thirty years. She inadvertently left her name on a joint credit card with her first husband. Several years ago—long after their divorce—he and his second wife filed for bankruptcy, which ultimately destroyed the perfect credit history Elaine had established. It's taken her five years to rebuild her credit history!

Beware of inquiries on your credit report

Inquiries are of two types—hard and soft. Too many hard inquiries in a short time can lower your score. Why? Because creditors may think you're having money troubles and searching for credit. And new accounts will lower your average account age, which could reduce your credit score.

What's a hard inquiry? It's when you authorize a lender to request a copy of your credit report. Every time you apply for credit, the creditor requests your credit report. Usually one credit inquiry will reduce your score by less than five points. But if you don't have very many accounts or you've got a short credit history, even one hard inquiry can have a bigger impact on your credit score. According to the Fair Isaac Corporation, "people with six inquiries or more on their credit reports can be up to eight times more likely to declare bankruptcy than people with no inquiries on their report." A lot of hard inquiries in a short time can have a much bigger impact on your credit score. Hard inquiries can stay on your credit report for up to two years.

When you're shopping for a mortgage loan or new car loan, you are probably triggering lenders to request your credit report. These are hard inquiries, but according to the Fair Isaac Corporation, multiple inquiries from mortgage lenders or automobile companies in a short time (thirty days) usually count as just one hard inquiry.

But how about when you're shopping at your favorite department store and you're offered a discount if you open a credit card account with the store? If you accept, it will request your credit report. Yep, another hard inquiry on your credit report. Just say, "No, thanks!"

So what's a soft inquiry? It's when you request your own credit report, and that does *not* affect your credit score. Other inquiries that don't affect your credit score include credit checks made by employers, lenders who want to offer you a "preapproved" credit card, or companies you're already doing business with that want to review your credit report.

I will request and review my credit report to do the following:

- Ensure my personal information is accurate

- Determine if the accounts listed belong to me

- Resolve any joint accounts with other people—ex-husband(s), children, or other relatives

- Discover old debts that need resolution

- Resolve any errors that I find

· PROFIT FROM HER STORY ·

Louisa says:
Be careful about credit accounts when you move!

"I tend to move every few years, and until I saw my credit report, I had no idea that some outstanding bills had gone to collection. One was a final bill from a cable company for $35, and another was a final bill from a long-distance company for a similar amount. Apparently those final bills never got forwarded to my new address, and I never missed them. And even though I didn't know about the collection efforts, I still got two very black marks against me. And even after I paid them, they can still remain on my credit reports for years! I did, however, add a letter to my file explaining the circumstances. This type of credit history problem can cause utility companies to require huge up-front deposits."

HOW TO CORRECT INACCURACIES

The Fair Credit Reporting Act (FCRA) promotes accuracy and ensures the privacy of information used in consumer reports. Both the credit-reporting agency and the company that provided the information to the credit-reporting agency, such as a credit card company or bank, have responsibilities for correcting inaccurate or incomplete information in your report. When making your corrections to your credit report, be sure to contact *both* the credit-reporting agency and the information provider and take the following steps:

1. Write the credit-reporting agency describing the information that's inaccurate. Send copies *(not originals)* of supporting documents. Clearly identify each item you dispute, state the facts, and explain why you dispute the information. Request deletion or correction, and include your name and address. Send your letter by certified mail, return receipt requested, to the credit-reporting agency and information provider. This verifies the date your letter is received. Keep copies of your letter and all documentation. The credit-reporting agency is required to investigate the item within thirty days. If your credit report contains erroneous information, the credit-reporting agency must correct it. Or if an item is incomplete, the credit-reporting agency must ensure it's completed. The credit-reporting agency must also forward all relevant data you provide about the dispute to the information provider. After the information provider receives notices of a dispute from the credit-reporting agency, it must investigate, review all relevant information, and report the results to the credit-reporting agency. The corrections are required to be done within thirty days. If the information provider finds the disputed information to be inaccurate, it must notify all nationwide credit-reporting agencies so they can correct the information in your file. When disputed information cannot be verified, it must be *deleted* from your file.

2. When the investigation is complete, the credit-reporting agency must give you the written results. If your dispute resulted in a change, it must also give you a free copy of

your credit report. If you don't hear from the credit-reporting agency within thirty days, contact it again using the process in step one.

3. Upon your request, the credit-reporting agency must send correction notices to anyone who received your report in the past six months. Job applicants can have a corrected copy of their report sent to anyone who received a copy during the past two years for employment purposes. If the investigation doesn't resolve your dispute, write your own version of events, and ask the credit-reporting agency to include your statement of dispute in your file and in future credit reports.

· PROFIT FROM HER STORY ·

Sheila says:
Your credit can be ruined by an evil twin!

"When I bought my house in 1995, the mortgage company found several accounts on my credit report that didn't belong to me. And they were delinquent accounts! It turns out there was someone else with my first name, middle initial, and last name. And I have an unusual name! I ended up paying a higher interest rate on my mortgage because there wasn't time to get my credit report corrected before we closed on my loan. Now I examine my credit report regularly to make sure it's correct."

SO WHAT'S YOUR NUMBER?

Did you know creditors use your credit score to determine whether to lend you money and at what interest rate? Potential employers review your credit report in making their determination on whether or not to hire you. Insurance companies use your credit score in determining your premiums, landlords may reject your rental application if your score is low, and utility companies may use your credit score to determine the amount of your deposit.

Many people don't realize the importance of their credit scores. My husband and I have always maintained good credit and knew it was an important factor in obtaining a mortgage, but until several years ago, we didn't realize our credit score determined the *interest rate* on our mortgage. That's because your credit score provides a measurement of your credit risk.

Most creditors and lenders use the credit-scoring model developed by Fair Isaac Corporation. However, there are many types of credit scores developed by independent companies, credit-reporting agencies, and lenders. The three major credit-reporting agencies determine your credit score using their own credit-scoring models, which is often confusing to consumers. Your credit score probably won't be the same if you request it from Experian, Equifax, and TransUnion because each company uses a slightly different credit-scoring model.

Credit scores range from 300 to about 850. Your FICO credit score is determined by using a variety of data from your credit report. The categories evaluated include: your payment history, length of credit history, amounts owed, new credit, types of credit used, and collections for bad debts.

What's a good credit score?

Most lenders consider credit scores above 700 as very good. The higher your credit score, the lower your risk, and a higher score saves you money, because you are then offered better interest rates. You're considered a higher risk if your score is below 600, which means you'll probably get approved for your loan but at a higher interest rate. The chart below (source: www.myfico.com, retrieved

January 8th, 2008) shows how improving your credit score can affect the interest rate on a $150,000 30-year, fixed-rate mortgage.

YOUR FICO SCORE	YOUR INTEREST RATE	MONTHLY PAYMENT
760–850	5.738%	$1,748
700–759	5.960%	$1,791
660–699	6.244%	$1,846
620–659	7.054%	$2,007
580–619	9.249%	$2,468
500–579	10.230%	$2,684

WHAT'S THE SECRET FORMULA?

Your FICO score improves through time when you manage your credit responsibly by paying your bills on time; keeping balances low on your credit cards; paying off your debt instead of moving it between credit cards; opening new credit cards *only* when you need them; regularly checking your credit reports for accuracy; and if you've missed payments, getting current and staying current.

Since the FICO credit score is the most commonly used model, let's consider the main factors used to determine it.

Payment history

Your payment history is worth approximately 35 percent of your score. Information considered includes:

- Payment information on credit cards, retail accounts, installment loans, and mortgage loans.

- Presence of adverse public records, including: bankruptcy, judgments, suits, liens, and wage attachments. Bankruptcies remain on your credit report for seven to ten years.

- Delinquent accounts and collection items, and how long they have been past due. Factors include: How late were your payments, how much did you owe, how many late payments did you have, and how recently did they occur? For example, if you made a payment last month that was sixty days overdue, it will affect your credit score more than a payment that was made ninety days late several years ago.

- Number of accounts that show no late payments. This is a *good thing* because it shows you have a good track record.

Amount you owe

The amount you owe is worth 30 percent of your score. Items considered include:

- Amount owed on all accounts. Even if you pay your credit cards off monthly, there will probably still be a balance on your credit report.

- What types of accounts have balances. Do you owe only on credit card or revolving accounts, or do you have an auto loan, mortgage loan, or installment loan?

- Number of accounts with balances. If you owe money on a large number of accounts, it could be an indication you're overextended.

- How much of your total credit line is being used. If you're close to maxing out your credit cards and revolving accounts, it could be an indication you'll have trouble making future payments.

- Proportion of installment amounts you still owe. For example, how much have you paid on the original amount borrowed on an automobile loan?

Credit history

The length of your credit history is worth approximately 15 percent of your score. What matters here is how long your accounts have been open and what kind of activity is shown. Having a bunch of accounts you don't use may not help your score. But if you have an account you've had for a long time, keep it! My husband and I maintain a credit card we've had for thirty years, which helps our score. Usually, a longer credit history *increases* your score.

New credit

Approximately 10 percent of your credit score is based on whether you're incurring new debt. Lenders look at how many accounts have been opened recently, how long it's been since you opened an account, and how many recent inquiries have been made. Here's where the number of *hard* inquiries can negatively affect your credit score. So next time you're in a department store and the clerk offers you 10 percent off your purchase if you open an account, just say, "No!" Is that 10 percent really worth it in the long run? Opening one new account may not affect your credit score, but opening several new accounts in a short time could affect it. Until I discovered how it could affect my credit score, I often opened new department store accounts just to receive the extra 10 percent off my purchases. Now I say, "No, thank you!"

Types of credit used

About 10 percent of your credit score is determined by the mixture of credit you have available—how many accounts you have and how many of each type. Categories include: credit cards, retail accounts, installment loans, and mortgages.

Frequently asked questions

Does credit counseling affect your credit score? The Fair Isaac Corporation doesn't consider credit counseling in determining your credit score. However, there are many other credit-scoring models that may consider it.

If my husband had bad credit before I was married, does that affect my credit score? If the credit account was held solely in the name of your spouse, it cannot affect your credit score. But do watch out for this—in community property states, all debt acquired during a marriage is considered a joint debt, regardless if the account is joint or in the name of an individual spouse, so beware if you live in one of those states.

WAYS TO IMPROVE YOUR CREDIT SCORE

- Consistently pay your bills on time. The longer you pay your bills on time the better. Time is an important factor that weighs heavily in all the credit-scoring agencies.

- Annually request, review, and correct your credit report.

- Keep balances low on your credit cards and other revolving debt. Don't use all your available credit.

- Avoid too many hard inquiries, because it may look as if you're seeking credit and could overextend yourself or you're having financial difficulties. This impression is especially important if you're shopping for a mortgage or automobile loan.

- Be cautious about moving your debt from one account to another to get a lower interest rate, especially if you're opening new accounts and closing accounts. Remember—opening new accounts creates hard inquiries.

- Pay off your credit cards and revolving debt; it's the best way.

You can increase your credit score by consistently taking these actions through long periods. Creditors are looking for low-risk behavior through time—the longer the better, and they reward those customers with the lowest interest rates and premiums.

I will improve my credit score by:

- Paying my bills consistently on time

- Maintaining no or low balances on my credit card accounts

- Thinking twice before opening a credit card account to get an extra 10 percent or 15 percent off my purchases

- Correcting any errors on my credit report(s) and following up to ensure the corrections have been made

Now that wasn't so bad, was it? Just remember to be vigilant. Now that you've cleaned up your credit report, you want to keep it that way. Next up: You'll learn how to safeguard yourself against some very bad guys who want to ruin your good name.

SEVEN

Get Smart about Protecting Your Identity

How to safeguard your financial house from thieves and intruders

---

Chapter Goals for You

- Understand how identity theft happens
- Evaluate how you use your credit and debit cards, and make adjustments as needed
- Get clear when to give out your Social Security number
- Consider how you deal with sensitive papers around your house
- Learn why there's a shredder in your future
- Discover what to do with unsolicited credit offers
- Secure your computer and online transactions
- Protect your incoming and outgoing mail

IT'S 11PM—DO YOU KNOW WHERE YOUR IDENTITY IS?

Identity theft is the fastest-growing white-collar crime in the United States, and it can happen to *anyone*. Several years ago a Brooklyn busboy stole the identities of numerous celebrities, including Oprah

Winfrey and Steven Spielberg. The Federal Trade Commission reports that ten million people are victims of identity theft each year, and that number is sure to grow. Even FTC Chairman Deborah Platt Majoras received a letter from shoe retailer DSW informing her that her credit card information had been stolen! It's a crime in which the victim must not only resolve the issue but also prove her innocence. Identity theft victims spend a long time and their own money cleaning up the mess identity thieves make. According to the Identity Theft Resource Center, victims spend an average of six hundred hours recovering from identity theft through a period of years, and they're out of pocket about $1,400. Approximately 85 percent of victims find out about the crime through an adverse situation—they were denied credit or employment, were notified by police or collection agencies, or they received bills for things they never ordered, and so on.

Identity theft is of two types: *account takeover* and *application fraud*. Account takeover occurs when an identity thief takes over your existing account information to buy products or services. Victims of account takeover usually learn about the fraud when they receive their monthly credit card statement. If you're lucky, your bank or credit card company may notice unusual activity on your account and call you to verify recent purchases. But even when it's an obvious case of fraud, it can still take months to rectify.

Application fraud is when the identity thief uses your Social Security number (SSN) and other identifying information to open new accounts in your name. It can be months before application fraud victims learn about the fraud, because monthly statements are sent to the thief's address. You probably won't learn of this until you check your credit report, you receive a call from a creditor, or a credit refusal leads you to investigate. It's another great reason to check your reports regularly. Even if you've used up your free reports for the year, the small fee for requesting another one is cheap insurance against a real nightmare.

· PROFIT FROM HER STORY ·

Lynn says:
Become more vigilant!

"There was a vague message on my voice mail from someone I'd never heard of, claiming to be from my bank. I actually thought that the message might be fraudulent, since I'd heard the horror stories about phone scams. So I wasn't in a hurry to return the call. Mistake Number One.

"It turns out the call was legit, and it was the credit card department at my bank monitoring suspicious activity on my debit card. In my case, the red-flag activity was a no-brainer: Some guy in Chile (yes, the South American country!) was indulging in a spending spree with my debit card. Then he made some unusual purchases but accidentally had them shipped to my address—which actually helped catch him.

"When I asked my bank how this could happen, I was told credit/debit card numbers were most often compromised at gas stations and restaurants, places that are notorious for high employee turnover and where your credit charge slips may be accessible to many people. The numbers are harvested and often sold in bulk to scammers in other countries, who believe they'll be immune to detection or prosecution.

"Although my bank restored the stolen money from my checking account within a week, it took several months to fully resolve the case. This experience has made me much more cautious about where I use my card. Especially when traveling, I now prefer to use cash for gas and food, and I use my card only where I have a high degree of trust in the place of business."

· PROFIT FROM HER STORY ·

Jody says:
Even your birthday is valuable information.

"I didn't even know someone was using my information to obtain credit until I got a phone call from the Verizon fraud department. It told me someone had applied for a new account with the company using my Social Security number, but the person was unable to verify my birthday. I then discovered the same person had used my information to obtain numerous credit cards and had spent thousands of dollars. I contacted the credit bureaus to put a fraud alert on my record, but it's been months, and I'm still trying to dig out from under this mess. Every time I think I've got it cleared up, another debt pops up. It's the most frustrating thing I've ever experienced!"

· PROFIT FROM HER STORY ·

Madeline says:
Be cautious about people coming to your door.

"A young man came to my front door one warm afternoon and asked if he could use my phone because his car had broken down. I felt sorry for him, so I brought the phone outside for him to use. I returned inside, locking my screen door but not closing the front door. Within minutes he was inside my house, had grabbed my purse, and was gone. I immediately called my bank to cancel my credit card and stop any transactions. But he had already used my card to fill his tank with gas. I'm thankful that's all he got. The worst thing was that I didn't listen to my little voice telling me to just say "No.""

NOW IS A GOOD TIME TO BE PARANOID

Although identity theft can happen to anyone, you can minimize your risk by managing your personal information wisely and cautiously with an awareness of the issue. Think of it like protecting your home. The house with a security system is less likely to be burglarized than the one next door with its windows left open.

Never give out your Social Security number without determining if it's really necessary. Your employer and financial institution need your Social Security number for wage and tax reporting. Other businesses may ask for your Social Security number for general record keeping, but whether or not you give it to them is *always* up to you. A video rental store asked for my Social Security number when it processed my application. I refused to give it out because the store didn't need it, and my application was still accepted. Whenever you give out personal information, always stop to consider how many people will have access to it, and evaluate the risks.

The Federal Trade Commission recommends you ask the following questions before giving out your Social Security number:

- Why do you need it?
- How will it be used?
- How do you protect it from being stolen?
- What law says I must give it to you?
- What will happen if I don't give it to you?

Never give your Social Security number to strangers over the phone, on the Internet, or by mail. Don't carry your Social Security card, credit cards, or other personal information you don't need in your wallet or purse. Imagine the consequences if these things are lost, stolen, or compromised. And don't carry your children's Social Security cards either. Do not write any PIN numbers on anything you carry around with you. You will need to show your Social Security card to an employer when you're starting a new job, and sometimes to financial institutions when you're applying for a loan. Otherwise, leave your Social Security card at home in a safe place.

· PROFIT FROM HER STORY ·

Gail says:
Guard your purse with your life!

"I didn't want to carry my heavy purse into the grocery store, so I took my debit card and left everything else behind. A thief broke into my car and stole my purse, which included my driver's license, checkbook, credit cards, Social Security card, and several other pieces of personal information. It was several months later when police pulled a local man over for a traffic stop and discovered piles of unopened mail, driver's licenses, and Social Security numbers in the backseat, including mine. After stealing my purse, the thief immediately started writing checks. And within a couple of days he had opened credit card accounts over the Internet in my name and racked up thousands of dollars in purchases. I've worked years to have good credit, and it was destroyed in an instant! I have already spent long hours trying to get my records corrected, and there's no end in sight."

More ways to protect your financial self

- Make a photocopy of the contents of your wallet in case your wallet is lost or stolen.

- Never include your driver's license or Social Security number on your checks. You're making your personal information available to anyone who sees your check.

- Shred credit card receipts and any other sensitive documents before you throw them away. Dumpster diving is a common method of identity theft.

- Keep items with personal information secured in a safe place in your home. Don't leave your purse or piles of mail lying around, particularly if you have roommates, employ outside help, or are having service work done in your home. I'm not suggesting that you be mistrusting of people you know, but roommates and even your teenager might invite someone into your home who has financial difficulties and is looking for an easy way to get money.

- Request your credit report free from each of the three major credit-reporting agencies: Equifax, Experian, and TransUnion. Visit the website at www.annualcreditreport.com or call (877) 322-8228. (Also see Chapter Six.)

- When you're verbally providing your personal information, ensure no one is eavesdropping.

Safety begins at your keyboard

To guard the safety of your online transactions, give personal information only at the secure sections of websites, because they scramble the information you send over the Internet. (Always look for the padlock icon, which will appear at the bottom of your browser when you are in the secure section of a website.) Phishing is a common method of identity theft. Identity thieves pretend to be a financial institution or company and send an email to get you to reveal your personal information. Don't open the email, and never click on links sent in unsolicited emails. If in doubt, contact the institution in question and ask if it sent you an email. PayPal, for example, has a whole department devoted to handling phishing scams. Here are some more tips:

- Consider password protecting your computer to prevent access by unauthorized people.

- Don't open or download files from strangers.

- Don't respond to suspicious emails. Delete them.

- Make sure you've enabled the firewall software built into your computer, which allows you to limit uninvited access to your computer.

- Also safeguard your computer by regularly updating your virus protection software—better yet, subscribe to one of the services that automatically updates your computer while you sleep.

- Don't discard a computer without destroying all the data on the hard drive.

- Don't discard or recycle a cell phone without completely erasing the data stored in your phone. The cell phone data eraser lets you choose the brand and model number of your cell phone and then displays the commands you need to delete every piece of data from it. Visit the website at www.wireless recycling.com.

Don't send out the invitation

Guard your mail from theft by installing a locked mailbox, but be sure to check with your local post office to find out what restrictions may apply. Or get a post office box or a box at a mail drop company, such as Mailboxes Etc.

If you decide to keep an unsecured mailbox, promptly remove mail after it's been delivered. Unsecured mail is a prime way that identity thieves can obtain your personal information. You can also replace paper bills and statements altogether with online versions.

Deposit outgoing mail only in post office collection boxes. Leaving your outgoing mail in your mailbox with the red flag up is a vivid invitation to identity thieves to help themselves to your mail. With one of your checks, they can use your account number and other information to create their own batch of checks to write against your hard-earned money.

Also, be alert for stolen mail. Review your monthly credit card statement to ensure there aren't any fraudulent charges. Pay attention to your billing cycles, and follow up with creditors if your bills don't arrive on time. A missing credit card statement could mean an identity thief is using your account and diverting mail to another address to cover his tracks. Just listen to the tales of mail woe from these four women.

• PROFIT FROM HER STORY •

Rachel says:
Don't tempt thieves!

"I got a call from a local grocery store because someone was trying to cash a check for $1,200 in my name. Someone had stolen a preapproved check from my mailbox. It was one of those checks that companies are always sending me, even though I don't request them. I'm so glad the grocery store called! Now I have a locked mailbox."

• PROFIT FROM HER STORY •

Paula says:
Beware of moving day and beyond!

"Last year we moved from an apartment to a house. I put in my change of address with the post office, but for some reason the post office didn't forward my mail to my new address. My mail was left lying near the mailboxes, so anyone could pick it up. Someone stole my mail, including my bank and credit card statements. What a mess!! I've got creditors calling me telling me I'm behind in my payments—on purchases I didn't make!"

· PROFIT FROM HER STORY ·

Ellen says:
You can't be too careful with your mail!

"I live in a rural area and thought I was smart by not having mail delivered to my home address. We have a post office box. But one day a neighbor who lives a couple of roads from us called me to let me know he had found our mail scattered all over his property. I was so disgusted! The only mail we received in our mailbox were those unsolicited, preapproved credit card applications and other miscellaneous junk mail. I completed the opt-out procedures online and called the post office to tell it I was removing my mailbox. The post office told me I couldn't do it, but I did it anyway and haven't had a problem since."

· PROFIT FROM HER STORY ·

Joanne says:
Watch out for cell phones with cameras!

"I went into a pizza restaurant to pick up an order I had called in. I paid by using my Visa check card, which, of course, is linked directly to my checking account. The young man behind the counter took my card, swiped it, and then laid it on the counter as he waited for the approval, which is pretty standard procedure. While he waited, he picked up his cell phone and started dialing. I noticed the phone, because it is the same model I have, but nothing seemed out of the ordinary. Then I heard a click that sounded like my phone sounds when I take a picture. He then gave me back my card but kept the phone in his hand as if he were still pressing buttons. Meanwhile, I'm thinking: *I wonder what he is*

▶

> *taking a picture of*, oblivious to what was really going on. Then it dawned on me: The only thing there was my credit card, so now I'm paying close attention to what he is doing. He set his phone on the counter, leaving it open. About five seconds later, I heard the chime that tells you that the picture has been saved. Now I'm standing there struggling with the fact that this boy just took a picture of my credit card. Yes, he played it off well, because had we not had the same kind of phone, I probably would never have known what happened. Needless to say, I immediately canceled that card as I was walking out of the pizza parlor and called the manager to report the employee's actions."

Credit offers and other junk mail to watch closely

Keep unsolicited, preapproved credit card offers out of your mail. You can "opt out" by calling (888) 567-8688 or visiting www.optoutprescreen.com, which is the consumer credit-reporting industry's opt-out website. It takes only a few minutes and drastically reduces unsolicited mail. You can opt out for two years, five years, or life. You'll need to provide your name, address, Social Security number, and date of birth. While you're on the phone, why not go ahead and opt out for all the other members of the household? The Direct Marketing Association (DMA) also assists consumers who prefer not to receive mail or telephone solicitations. Visit the DMA website at www.dmaconsumers.org/consumerassistance.html. It charges a $1 fee to get your name off the lists, but believe me, it's worth it! You'll be removed from the lists for five years, and your junk mail will be drastically reduced.

Stop the unsolicited promotional offers that include checks from your own credit card companies by calling their customer service phone numbers. Tell them you don't wish to receive those offers.

If you make a donation to a nonprofit organization, you're probably on its mailing list forever. If you don't want to receive the mailings, write a note and put it in the next self-addressed envelope you receive from the organization. You'll receive less mail, and you'll save the organization money.

If you want to stop those annoying telemarketing phone calls, log on to www.donotcall.gov. Your registration will be effective for five years, and most telemarketers will stop calling you once your name has been on the list for a month. If you still continue to receive phone calls, you can file a complaint with the Federal Trade Commission.

Never throw those credit card solicitations unopened into the trash! Shred them or burn them—think of them as if they were actual credit cards. Identity thieves often use preapproved credit to obtain credit cards and make purchases. The thieves will simply request that the new credit cards be sent to *their* address. They are then able to use the credit cards for several months while the victim is completely unaware. Identity theft victims usually don't find out until the creditors begin calling about late payments.

The best kind of shredder to have is the newer cross-cut type that cuts your papers in two directions, with the end result looking more like confetti than the spaghetti strips the older shredders make. Believe it or not, determined thieves have been known to piece back together documents that were shredded the old way!

> **· PROFIT FROM HER STORY ·**
>
> *Carol* says:
> Save your receipts and study your bills!
>
> "A couple of years ago I got my monthly Visa bill and was comparing my receipts to the charges on the bill. I discovered two purchases for less than $45 that appeared to be bought online. I hadn't made either of the purchases, so I immediately called Visa. It said it would investigate the charges and advise me of the status within thirty days. I said I wanted to close the account and open a new account with a new number, because I had no idea who had my credit card number."

WHAT TO DO IF YOU'RE A VICTIM OF IDENTITY THEFT

The Federal Trade Commission provides a wealth of detailed information on identity theft on its websites: www.ftc.gov or www.consumer.gov/idtheft. Its online publication *Deter, Detect, Defend* explains how to protect yourself from identity theft and what actions to take if you're a victim of identity theft. The publication also includes an ID Theft Affidavit, which you can send to the credit-reporting agencies if a new account was opened in your name. Other identity theft resources include:

Privacy Rights Clearinghouse
www.privacyrights.org

Identity Theft Resource Center
www.idtheftcenter.org

- If you have reason to believe you are a victim of identity theft, your first step is to immediately contact the three major credit-reporting agencies (Experian, Equifax, and TransUnion) to have a fraud alert put on your credit record. The fraud alert requires creditors to contact you before opening any new accounts or making any changes to your existing accounts. It also provides you with free copies of yourcredit report.

- Next, close the new accounts that have been opened in your name or the accounts you believe have been compromised. Call the security department of each company to notify it of the fraud. You'll want to follow up in writing and send copies of supporting documents.

- File a complaint with your local police department and ask for a copy of the report.

- Complete the ID Theft Affidavit, which is available on the Federal Trade Commission website. Ask the FTC to verify in writing when the fraudulent debt has been discharged.

- Keep a folder with the copies of all documentation and a log to record your conversations. At a minimum, the log should include company contacted, the name of the person you talked with, the date, the time, and what you were told.

- Last, but definitely not least, file a complaint with the Federal Trade Commission. This can be done online at www.ftc.gov/idtheft or by calling (877) 438-4338.

FIND OUT WHERE YOUR IDENTITY IS

You have multiple ways to protect yourself against those who would steal your identity.

> **Circle the actions you plan to take to safeguard yourself against identity theft.**
>
> O Take my Social Security card out of my wallet
>
> O Remove unnecessary personal information from my wallet
>
> O Order new checks without my driver's license or Social Security number
>
> O Photocopy everything in my wallet
>
> O Request and review my credit reports from the three major credit-reporting agencies
>
> O Opt out of unsolicited, preapproved credit cards by calling (888) 567-8688 or visiting www.optoutprescreen.com and the Direct Marketing Association at www.dmaconsumers .org/consumerassistance.html
>
> O Install a locked mailbox or open a post office box
>
> O Stop leaving outgoing mail in my mailbox
>
> O Buy a cross-cut shredder
>
> O Shred all my credit card receipts and other sensitive documents
>
> O Review my monthly credit card statements
>
> O Install virus protection software on my computer and run it regularly
>
> O Stop opening email attachments from people I don't know

Before long, you should know the answer to the question: Do you know where your identity is? In the next chapter, we'll start thinking ahead and planning your financially secure future. Won't that be a relief?!

EIGHT

Get Ready for Your Financial Future

How to make sure you are prepared for
all events, both large and small

Chapter Goals for You

· Start a contingency fund

· Start an emergency fund

· Begin saving with automatic deductions

· Evaluate your financial needs for retirement and
fund your pension plans

· Learn about and open an IRA

· Understand why Social Security is important

NOW YOU'RE READY TO THINK AHEAD

If you've made it this far, you're well on your way to getting your
financial house in order. So now it's time to examine what prepa-
rations you've made for your later years. (Assuming you don't want
to work until you drop dead over your keyboard!) Some of you are
already making strides in this area, while others need to play catch-
up. Retirement can be a wonderful time of your life, full of opportunities for self-expression that got sidetracked while you were busy

earning a living and raising a family. But like most good things, it takes a lot of preparation.

· PROFIT FROM HER STORY ·

Cathy says:
Saving is good for your mental health!

"As I look back just one year ago, I am amazed at how far Bob and I have come. Our finances are in order, we've lowered our debt, we're talking about finances regularly (in a positive manner), and our thinking about money has completely changed. A prime example is when Bob wanted to buy a new motorcycle. Rather than just get a loan, we decided to buy an investment that would provide enough passive income to make a bike payment.

"We were able to find rental property that ended up providing enough income to buy two used motorcycles. We did finance the bikes but have already paid them off, and the rentals continue to produce passive income. Contrast that with how we used to think. Had Bob wanted a new motorcycle a few years ago, we would have financed a brand-new one. We would still be paying on it, and we wouldn't have the income from the property working for us.

"A couple of months ago, Bob's company went on strike. Several years ago when we thought his company might go on strike, we had only $2,000 in savings. I was a nervous wreck because I wondered how we would survive financially. The strike didn't happen, and can you guess what we did with the $2,000 we'd saved? We spent it.

"It wasn't until attending the forum that I realized how important it was to establish an emergency savings account again (and that we needed more than $2,000 in it). It's a good thing too, because without the savings we have, we'd be borrowing money to ▶

---

get through this strike. We don't know how long it will last, but we have a lot more savings and less debt this time. It's a good feeling, and I'm not having anxiety attacks like I had several years ago (when the strike didn't even occur).

"In fact, in the last year we've put more than $14,000 into savings for emergencies and vacations. We've developed a debt-reduction plan and have paid down $17,500 in debt (this is in addition to what we've saved). We also paid $9,000 cash for a good used car (rather than buy a new one). We were able to do all of this because I went back to work full time in September 2004 after a year of part-time work. Rather than increase our spending back to previous levels, we lived on half my salary. The other half went to savings and paying off debt. I still can't believe the difference it's made in just one short year."

Just grit your teeth, tighten your purse strings, and do it!

There's no escaping this fact: If you spend all the money you earn—or more!—you can't prepare for any kind of financially secure future. As painful as it may be to many of you, it is essential to save part of your income every month. We're not good with delayed gratification in this country; we require ever-faster electronic devices to speed up the pace of our lives, and quaint ideas such as Christmas savings clubs and layaway plans are seldom used anymore. So it's no surprise that the thought of setting aside a substantial part of your income while still in your twenties or thirties is unappealing to many people. It's been said that "retirement" is not even a concept to people in their twenties. But the truth is, the sooner you start, the easier it is, because the longer your money works for you, the less you'll have to work for your money.

Before we go any further, you need to understand the difference between saving and investing. Saving money won't make you rich, but it will be there when you need it. Savings are your security. Investments (stocks, bonds, mutual funds, etc.) involve risk. If you make good investment decisions, your investments will yield higher returns through time than savings. I recommend you have a combination of both savings and investments; however, I'm not going to go into great detail about investments, because it's beyond the scope of this book. To learn more about investments, check out the resources listed in this book and on my website (www.money wisewomen.net or through www.marciabrixey.com), or consult a financial professional (see Chapter Ten).

· PROFIT FROM HER STORY ·

Rona says:
Start young, retire happy!

"My parents have no investment background, so I grew up thinking that having a savings account is the only way to invest. I've been given enough information to be comfortable with investing in mutual funds, CDs, stocks, and so on. I feel very fortunate to be provided this information while still young. So not only will I have a 401(k) and stocks, mutual funds, and so on, but I don't have to worry about getting enough Social Security when I retire forty years from now."

You must create a contingency fund

Yes, really! You need to have money set aside in a contingency fund with relatively easy access for unexpected or irregular expenses, such as car repairs, a large vet bill, minor repairs on your house, money to send your children to summer camp, and so on.

I didn't have a contingency fund until I started on my own journey to financial fitness. Whenever I had an unexpected expense, I just said, "Charge it!" Does this sound familiar? Once I had my contingency fund in place, it reduced my need to charge unexpected expenses. And it will do the same thing for you. The amount you have in your contingency fund depends on your personal situation. Things to consider include age and condition of your home, appliances, automobiles, children's expenses, and so on; how often these type of expenses crop up; and your own comfort level with the unknown.

You also need an emergency fund

It's best to have both a contingency *and* an emergency fund. Yes, two different funds. So what's the difference? An emergency fund is for big-time situations such as losing your job, having major surgery, a personal property loss (a fire or flood in your home), and so on. Most experts recommend you keep between three and six months' worth of your net income in your emergency account.

Where and how to stash it—not under your mattress!

Your emergency fund should be accessible, but not so easily accessible that you dip into it frequently. There are numerous places to keep your contingency and emergency funds that provide you with a small return; these are accessible but don't have supereasy access. They include: certificates of deposit (CDs), U.S. Savings Bonds, savings accounts, and money market accounts—all of which are available through financial institutions. They offer access to your money at a low risk, but they don't pay a high interest rate.

Certificates of deposit offer a higher interest rate and a bit less access. A strategy called laddering allows you to earn the highest possible interest on your CDs and still have access to your money. Let's say you have $5,000 to save for one of your funds. Put $1,000 each into a one-, two-, three-, four-, and five-year CD. Usually the CD with the longer maturity date earns a higher interest rate. When your one-year CD matures, it will pay $1,000 plus interest. If you don't need the money, reinvest it in a five-year CD. Repeat this process each year as the next CD matures. This laddering strategy provides a CD that matures every year, yet it always has you investing in a new five-year CD with your $1,000 plus interest. If you need to withdraw the money before the next CD matures, you will just be required to pay an interest penalty. Depending on the interest rates at the time, you may decide to ladder your CDs for a shorter time.

Buying U.S. Savings Bonds online or through payroll deduction is a simple and easy way to save money for your emergency fund. There are two different savings bonds: EE Bond and I Bond. The minimum holding period is twelve months, which means you must wait twelve months before you can cash a bond. You'll lose three months' interest if you don't hold on to your bond for at least five years from the issue date. The Treasury Department has made it even easier to buy U.S. Savings Bonds. If you open a Treasury Direct account, you can buy electronic savings bonds automatically online. You can also convert your paper savings bonds to electronic bonds, which prevents your bonds from getting lost. To learn more, visit www.treasurydirect.gov.

You can also keep your emergency fund in a savings or money market account. Savings accounts pay interest, but usually not at a very high rate. You can withdraw your money at any time. Money market accounts generally pay a higher interest rate than savings accounts because your money is invested in CDs and U.S. Treasury bills.

I don't recommend establishing your emergency fund in the financial institution you use regularly, because these days it's incredibly easy to transfer money between your accounts. It can be done online, by phone, or in person. It's just too easy! Establish the emergency fund in a financial institution that's across town or in another city. Make it difficult to get to your money and your chances of not dipping into the fund will significantly improve. Take it from someone who's been there. We opened our emergency fund in a money market account in another state. To withdraw money, we had to write at least a $500 check. As a result, we rarely withdraw money from our emergency fund.

Now, if you're wondering how you're going to establish and maintain both these funds while paying your monthly bills, take one small step at a time. The easiest, most painless way to establish your contingency and emergency funds is to have the money automatically and regularly withheld from your paycheck. If your employer doesn't offer this option, or if you're self-employed, have the money automatically withdrawn from your bank account. If you don't see it, you won't miss it, and you won't spend it.

· PROFIT FROM HER STORY ·

Nancy says:
Save it, but hide it!

"I have money from my paycheck automatically deposited into a savings account in a different bank from where my regular checking and savings accounts are. The bank is across town, and it's harder for me to get there to withdraw the money."

· PROFIT FROM HER STORY ·

Laurie says:

Never saw it, never missed it!

"I have a savings account, which is strictly for property taxes and insurance. My husband and I determine the annual amounts due and convert them to biweekly payments. We have that amount withheld from our paychecks and automatically deposited into our savings account. Whenever our property taxes and insurance increase, we simply make adjustments to the amount withheld. We never have to worry about how we're going to come up with money to pay these expenses."

Fill in the action steps you plan to take.

- I have already established my contingency fund at

  _____.

- There is $_____ in my contingency fund.

- I will establish a contingency fund by (date) _____ and fund it by having $_____ automatically withheld from my paycheck or bank account.

- I have already established my emergency fund at

  _____.

- There is $_____ in my emergency fund.

- I will establish an emergency fund by (date) _____ and fund it by having $_____ automatically withheld from my paycheck or bank account.

- There is $_____ in my emergency fund, which is about (number of) _____ months of living expenses.

DON'T LEAVE YOUR FUTURE TO
CHANCE OR WILLPOWER

We've all heard the saying "Pay yourself first." But what does it mean? It's not just an external action; it's realizing that you're important, and you deserve to get paid first. We all work hard for our money; why shouldn't we get paid first? Somewhere along the journey of life, many of us—especially women—have moved ourselves to the back of the line. Maybe it goes back to our caregiving and nurturing tendencies—taking care of everyone but ourselves. Or it might be because we think we're selfish if we pay ourselves first. Let's rephrase our thinking—think of "paying yourself first" as taking control of your road to financial independence. Begin by pulling out your most recent pay stub. Look at the money that's coming out of your paycheck *before* you get paid. All those sources are getting paid before you. Think about it—don't you deserve to "pay yourself first"? The best way to accomplish this is to contribute to your company's 401(k) plan—if it has one. If you can't afford to contribute the maximum amount, start small, but start— and start now! Every time you get a raise, cost of living increase, or extra income, increase your contribution until you reach the maximum. Trust me—it works! And every time you review your pension plan statement and watch how your money has grown, you'll experience the feeling of power and know that you're moving along on your road to financial independence. If your company doesn't have a 401(k) plan, fund an individual retirement account (IRA). Remember, start small if necessary, but start, and start now!

Employer pension plans—401(k), or 403(b) for nonprofit organizations—allow employees to contribute part of their salaries to these plans. This type of pension plan is called a defined contribution plan, because contributions are made by your employer, yourself, or both. Enroll and begin contributing as much as the plan allows, as soon as you can. If you can't afford to contribute the maximum amount, start small and contribute what you can. Increase your contribution whenever you can. Funding your company retirement plan is one of the most important steps you can take to ensure you have a financially secure future. Many employers match a percentage of your contribution, and you don't pay taxes on your contributions or any of the earnings until you use them. Your employer's contribution is *free* money. Who wouldn't want free money? Take a minute to think about this: If someone offered you a $100 bill, would you turn her down? No way! So don't say, "No," to your employer if you're offered a retirement plan with a matching percentage. The beauty of the company retirement plan is that the money is withheld from your paycheck, so you never see it or miss it.

I think this is a no-brainer, but I can't tell you how many people I've met who aren't contributing to their pension plans. Their (literally) poor excuses include:

- I can't afford it.
- Why should I contribute when my employer doesn't match my contribution?
- I just haven't taken the time to complete the paperwork.
- I don't know where to invest my money. (Employees are intimidated by the idea of managing their own money, so they procrastinate.)
- My husband takes care of this.

Some employees have the option to invest in mutual funds or company stock, but be cautious about investing all your funds in company stock. Remember the Enron employees? Their retirement funds weren't diversified—they were all invested in Enron stock. And one day it all went poof.

So what's diversification? It simply means investing your money in various types of financial assets to distribute varying degrees of risk, such as stocks, bonds, mutual funds, and certificate of deposits. Assets that have the potential to pay a higher amount on your investment are usually a higher risk, while investments with a smaller earning potential have less risk. Using the Enron employees as an example, their retirement funds could have been diversified by investing part in mutual funds and part in the company stock; this would have reduced their risk.

The Pension Protection Act of 2006 encourages employers to use automatic enrollment to increase employee participants in 401(k) and 403(b) plans. If an employee for one reason or another fails to elect participation in a plan, the employer can automatically enroll her. This is a good thing, especially for employees who haven't taken the necessary action to contribute to their pension plan. However, you'll still need to do your homework to determine how your money is invested.

My husband and I both contributed the maximum to the federal government's Thrift Savings Plan, which is equivalent to a 401(k). Our contributions, combined with the magic of compounding interest, grew quickly. But back in the mid-1980s, we didn't spend the time to educate ourselves on the various ways to invest our money. We left it in the fund with the least amount of risk. Why? Ignorance! We lost about ten years of investing our money in funds with greater growth potential. That being said, we still made a very wise decision to contribute the maximum to our pension plan. Our money still grew, just not as much as it would have if we had invested in a more aggressive fund. So I want you to know that you're not alone. You've got to have the desire to be financially independent, take the steps to get educated, take action. I did it, and you can too!

The other type of pension plan is the *defined benefit plan,* better known as the *traditional plan,* which pays you a guaranteed monthly benefit as long as you live. This type of pension plan is quickly disappearing. According to one source, twenty years ago, 40 percent of American workers were covered by defined benefit plans, and now it's only about 20 percent.

In May 2005, United Airlines defaulted on its pension obligations to retirees and workers, and other companies are following suit. What exactly does this mean? To United Airline workers, it means their monthly pensions will be reduced anywhere from 20 to 50 percent!

· PROFIT FROM HER STORY ·

Leah says:

I feel vaguely anxious all the time!

"My husband and I both work for the county, have no kids, live in a great house in San Clemente, scuba dive, and take fantastic vacations. We don't have enough in our emergency fund, and it seems so overwhelming (the amount of money required for this fund) that I just feel vaguely anxious about it all the time! Oh, and I'm consumed by worry about our pensions' failing. The advice to open a Roth sounds good, but I feel that it's all just too overwhelming! Between saving for that fund, funding a retirement, and maxing out our deferred compensation, I feel like there just isn't enough to go around and still enjoy life. Aarrrgghh!"

Are you, like Leah, wondering how you can protect yourself? Don't live in fear, but plan accordingly. Each time you get a raise, cost of living increase, or promotion, increase your contribution to your retirement fund. An alternative way is to write an action plan to schedule your contribution increases. In no time at all, you'll be contributing the maximum and won't even miss the money! You can think of your IRAs and other investments as a kind of insurance—just in case something happens to your pension.

THE INS AND OUTS OF IRAS

In addition to your company-sponsored retirement plans, you might also want to establish an individual retirement account (IRA). IRAs are not as complicated or complex as you might think. But keep in mind that they are *individual* retirement accounts, which means they are not jointly owned. Why is this important? Because if you are married and your spouse contributes to his IRA, but you don't have an IRA of your own, you may end up out of luck later on. (I'll talk more about this under spousal IRAs.) Anyone under the age of seventy and a half with earned income may contribute to a traditional or Roth IRA. There are several types of IRAs.

Traditional IRA

This may be tax deductible, depending on your modified adjusted gross income and whether you or your spouse participate in a qualified retirement plan through your employer. The earnings in your traditional IRA are always tax deferred, which means you won't pay taxes on the earnings until you begin withdrawing the money, which you can begin doing at age fifty-nine and a half. You must start taking distribution of a traditional IRA by age seventy and a half.

Roth IRA

Unlike with a traditional IRA, your contribution to a Roth is *not* tax deductible; it's taxed in the year of contribution. However, the *earnings* you accumulate in a Roth IRA are never taxed when used for retirement income. For example, let's say you contributed $50,000 to your Roth IRA during a twenty-year period. When you start withdrawing from your IRA, it's valued at $85,000, which means your earnings were $35,000. *None* of the money you receive from a Roth is taxable, because you already paid taxes on your contributions, and the earnings aren't taxable. Another difference from a traditional IRA is that a Roth doesn't require you to take distributions when you reach seventy and a half, so it can continue to grow until you need it.

Spousal IRA

If you're married and a stay-at-home mom, you're working—just not getting paid for your work. If your husband is working, he can contribute to a spousal IRA. In 2008 your spouse can contribute up to $5,000 annually if you're under age fifty. Do you think that sounds like a lot of money? Let's look at $5,000 as your annual salary for your job as stay-at-home mom. If we consider forty hours a week, your hourly wage is less than $3 per hour. Don't you think you deserve it? Yes, you do! Respect and protect yourself, and contribute the maximum to a spousal IRA. Be sure to check with the IRS to find out how much you can contribute in any given year.

Savings Incentive Match Plan for Employees (SIMPLE)

This is an IRA established by a small employer for the company employees. It's similar to a 401(k) plan. Employees contribute a percentage of their salaries and receive a percentage from their employer. Consult with a professional before deciding which plan is best for you.

Or you can do it yourself

If you're self-employed, you can save for your retirement with a Simplified Employee Pension Plan (SEP) IRA. The maximum contribution increases regularly, so consult with the IRS for the latest limits. SEPs are as easy to establish as a traditional or Roth IRA, but you can make much larger contributions each year. And they're tax deductible.

More considerations

If you have property with a named beneficiary, it bypasses the instructions in your will. This includes life insurance, retirement accounts, tax-deferred annuities, U.S. Savings Bonds, and bank accounts in trust for others. I'll talk more about this in Chapter Nine.

Beware: If you withdraw any of your IRA before age fifty-nine and a half, you may have to pay a 10 percent penalty on the earnings, plus pay income tax on the money you take out. One way to avoid the penalty is an IRS tax code item called 72(t). It allows you to take your IRA out as defined by the IRS in "substantially equal and periodic payments that are based on life-expectancy tables."

Carol tapped into this provision after accepting a buyout from her employer at age fifty-five. The 72(t) provision provided her with the monthly income she needed to meet her monthly living expenses. Be sure to consult a financial professional for guidance with the 72(t) rule.

· PROFIT FROM HER STORY ·

Janice says:
Think twice before withdrawing money
from your company retirement plan early!

Janice's husband, Greg, quit his job, and they desperately needed money to pay their household expenses, so he decided to withdraw the money in his company retirement plan. Neither Janice nor Greg realized that in addition to the 10 percent penalty, the money would be considered income on their tax return. Imagine their surprise when they did their income taxes and discovered they owed the IRS $10,000—which they had to go into debt to pay!

Can you still contribute to an IRA if you don't work? Unfortunately not—with one exception: the spousal IRA I talked about earlier. You must have earned income to contribute to an IRA. Earned income is defined as wages, commissions, bonuses, tips, self-employment income, and fees for professional services.

> ### · PROFIT FROM HER STORY ·
> #### *Melissa* says:
> #### Take a second job if you need to!
>
> "I've been working as a substitute teacher for more than three years. I just got hired on as a permanent employee and will be selecting my retirement plan based on what I've learned at the forum. I'll be putting away as much pretax money as I can. I want to make thoughtful, conscious decisions around how I structure my finances. I've also looked at ways to increase my income, since I have already trimmed my expenditures as much as possible. I've started teaching Spanish two evenings a week to supplement my income, and I want to put those extra earnings into an IRA fund. Now when I go to work at my evening job, I'll know I'm doing something wonderful for myself, and it's worth the extra effort."

My IRA experience

In 1996 I decided I wanted to fund an IRA, but I didn't have the extra money to regularly contribute. So I called our cable TV company and reduced our cable service to basic service, which saved us $30 per month. I took this extra money and established a traditional IRA in a certificate of deposit at our credit union.

The monthly contribution was automatically withdrawn from our checking account. Several years later we met with a financial adviser, who asked why we had an IRA established in a certificate of deposit paying less than 3 percent interest. I can still remember my response: "Is there any other way?" The financial adviser explained that an IRA can be invested in any number of approved investments, including mutual funds, stocks, bonds, or real estate.

Most of these investments have the potential to pay more than 3 percent on your investment. Although I could have beat myself up for investing my IRA in a low interest–bearing certificate of deposit, I didn't do that. Instead, I congratulated myself on the fact that I had taken the initiative to open and regularly fund an IRA.

· PROFIT FROM HER STORY ·

Mary says:
Do your homework, and understand
your options for all eventualities!

Although they were comfortably retired, Mary and her husband, Joe, were unprepared for what happened to them. When Joe had a stroke last year, he also suffered a personality change. After a couple of stays in a convalescent home, which drained the couple's assets, Joe announced he wanted to move in with their adult daughter. This daughter then quickly took control of her father's finances, including his pension, Social Security benefits, and IRAs. Mary was left with only her own monthly Social Security benefits, which are minimal because she never worked outside the home. What Mary didn't realize was that IRAs are *not* joint assets. Therefore, she couldn't touch any of the funds in Joe's IRAs. Unfortunately, Mary couldn't turn the clock back to fund a spousal IRA for herself. Mary also didn't realize that Joe could have funded a spousal IRA for her while he was working.

Fill out this action plan, and stick to it!

If you are an employee:

- My company-sponsored retirement plan allows me to contribute _____%.

- I am contributing the maximum of _____%.

- I am contributing _____%, which is not the maximum.

- I have devised an action plan to contribute the maximum by _____ (date).

If you are self-employed:

- I am contributing $_____ annually to a SEP IRA.

- I am contributing $_____ annually to an individual IRA.

- I have established a SIMPLE IRA for my employees and myself.

IRA:

- I have established an Individual Retirement Account (IRA).

- I am contributing $_____ per month, or $_____ annually, to my IRA.

- My IRA is (circle one): Traditional IRA, ROTH IRA, Spousal IRA

Resources for IRAs

The Motley Fool
www.fool.com

Internal Revenue Service
www.irs.gov

MAKE YOUR MONEY WORK EXTRA HARD FOR YOU

The best description of dollar cost averaging I've ever read is in the book *It's More Than Money, It's Your Life*. According to Candace Bahr and Ginita Wall, "Dollar cost averaging is a fancy term for investing money on a regular basis." This is exactly what you want to do. So now it's time to go back to Chapter Four to determine how much you can regularly invest, and to complete the statement below.

{ I will begin investing $_____ per (week or month). }

Here's the best part about investing: compounding interest. I think compounding interest is magic. Even Albert Einstein thought it was the eighth wonder of the world! Understanding the power of compounding interest is a gift we give to ourselves, to our children, and to any other young people in our lives. I wish someone had explained it to me when I was in my twenties.

Several years ago when I gave up my morning latte and switched to drip coffee, I saved $2 a day, $10 a week, $520 a year. It was a painless way to find $10 a week. Now, let's look at what I could have done with that $10 a week if I had started saving it when I was twenty and invested it at an 8 percent growth rate. I'd have $228,563 when I turn sixty-five. I think that's a *wow!* When I share this information in my forums, women often tell me this information is depressing because they're not in their twenties, but in their forties or fifties.

But don't get depressed, because it's never, never, never too late to start investing. Even if you start at age forty-five and save $10 a week at an 8 percent growth rate, you'll still have $25,524 at age sixty-five. And that's a great increase, because your total investment was only $5,460. Check out the chart below to get inspired.

Look how much your retirement account will be at age sixty-five with the following weekly investments at a hypothetical 8 percent annual growth rate.

AGE	$10	$25	$50	$100	$150
20	$228,563	$571,408	$1,142,817	$2,285,634	$3,428,451
30	$99,402	$248,504	$497,008	$994,016	$1,491,024
35	$64,582	$161,456	$322,911	$645,822	$968,734
40	$41,211	$103,028	$206,056	$412,111	$618,167
45	$25,524	$63,811	$127,621	$255,242	$382,863
50	$14,995	$37,487	$74,975	$149,950	$224,925
55	$7,928	$19,819	$39,638	$79,277	$118,915

There are several things to know about compounding interest:

- No amount is too small to invest.
- Start investing young, but if that train has left the station, start now!
- Invest regularly and automatically. Making it automatic is a must! We all have good intentions, but if the money is in our regular account, we'll probably spend it.

Now that we've talked about the steps you can personally take to prepare for a secure financial future, let's talk about something that you've probably heard about—Social Security. You might be wondering why you should bother to read about Social Security, because it probably won't be there when you need it. Think again and read on.

THE INS AND OUTS OF SOCIAL SECURITY

What do you think when you think about Social Security?

- Don't count on it, because it won't be there.
- I think about retirement and old people.
- It's going broke.
- Social Security takes a lot of money out of my paycheck.

I heard all this and much more during the twenty-six years I worked for the Social Security Administration. The one thing I know for sure is that Social Security is the backbone of our country. I don't believe it will ever disappear. But it will look different from how it does today. The program and benefits have changed a lot through the years. There have been a variety of changes: elimination of student benefits; the $255 lump sum death payment is paid only to widows or children; Social Security benefits are taxed; and the full retirement age has been raised to age sixty-seven. And those are just the things I can remember—I'm sure there are more. My point is that Social Security will survive—but don't think for one minute that your monthly Social Security benefit will sustain your current lifestyle. No way! Nor was it ever meant to. According to the Women's Institute for a Secure Retirement, older women are twice as likely as elderly men to be living near or below the federal poverty threshold.

Social Security isn't just a retirement benefit; it's a package of protection for you and your family. For an average worker with a spouse and two children, survivor's benefits are equal to a $403,000 life insurance policy and a $353,000 disability policy.

The cover of the February 25, 2002 issue of *People* magazine showed a picture of thirty-one women who had babies after their husbands died in the events of September 11, 2001. This is a sad but graphic example of how Social Security survivor's benefits help your loved ones financially. If their husbands had paid into Social Security long enough, the widows and their children were eligible for Social Security. Survivor's benefits are paid to children until age eighteen, and this may also include stepchildren or adopted children. A widow may be eligible for benefits if she is taking care of the deceased's child, as long as the child is under age sixteen or is disabled and receiving Social Security benefits.

· PROFIT FROM HER STORY ·

Dolly says:

Social Security helped me raise my granddaughter!

Dolly was surprised that she was able to get some relief in her situation.

"Our daughter, Jill, died when her only child, Jessica, was three months old. Jill was only twenty-two and hadn't worked very much. The good thing was that she had contributed enough into the Social Security system to provide a monthly survivor's benefit for Jessica. The monthly benefit isn't much, but it's helping me provide for Jessica's needs until she turns eighteen."

There are a number of different kinds of available Social Security benefits that people are not commonly aware of. The following sections address these benefits in detail.

Disability benefits

According to Merriam-Webster's dictionary, disability is the "inability to pursue an occupation because of a physical or mental impairment." The definition Social Security uses expands on this, because the program pays benefits only to people who are totally disabled. They don't pay benefits to people with a partial or short-term disability. You're considered disabled if you can't do the work you did previously, and it's determined you can't adjust to other work because of your medical conditions. In addition, your disability must be expected to last, or has already lasted, for at least one year, or is expected to result in your death.

Retirement benefits

Now you know that Social Security is not just about your retirement benefits. And speaking of those, the full retirement age is no longer age sixty-five. For anyone born 1960 or later, your full retirement age is sixty-seven. You can still receive reduced benefits at age sixty-two, but the reduction in your monthly benefit will be higher. The age to qualify for the Medicare benefit remains age sixty-five.

Social Security uses your highest thirty-five years of earnings to determine your retirement benefit. Not the highest three years or five years, like many pensions, but the highest thirty-five years. Think about that, and let it sink in; that's a long time! Remember that women are often out of the workplace for an average of fifteen years, which means the years with low earnings or no earnings are counted as zero earning years to bring the total years of earnings to thirty-five years. This is why a woman's average monthly Social Security benefit is about $200 less a month than a man's benefit. We've already talked about spousal IRAs, which is one way to cover yourself while you're not working outside the household.

Spousal benefits

There are numerous types of benefits for spouses. Although I'm going to talk about women, Social Security benefits are gender neutral—these same benefits apply to men. If your husband dies, you can receive widow's benefits if you are age sixty or older; if you are age fifty or older and disabled; or if you're caring for a child who is under age sixteen or disabled and entitled to benefits. You may be eligible for divorced spouse benefits if your marriage lasted ten years or longer, you're now unmarried, you're age sixty-two or older, and your Social Security benefit is not higher than one-half of your ex-husband's unreduced benefits. So if you're about ready to file your final divorce papers and you've been married only nine and a half years, *stop* and wait for six more months. I'm not telling you to live with your soon-to-be ex-husband; just don't make your divorce final.

If your ex-husband has *not* applied for benefits but can qualify for them and is age sixty-two or older, you may receive benefits on his record if you have been divorced from him for at least two years and meet the above requirements. I've talked to attorneys who didn't know about this benefit. It's the only Social Security benefit I'm aware of in which the wage earner is still alive and not receiving benefits, yet a divorced spouse can receive a monthly benefit. I believe this benefit was established to protect the women who were married for twenty to thirty years, didn't work outside the household, and found themselves unable to find jobs with good salaries because they didn't have work experience. If you're divorced, be sure to keep your ex-husband's Social Security number, your original or certified copy of your marriage certificate, and your divorce decree. And for those of you who burned any or all of those documents, it's time to get a certified copy for your records. You'll need those documents when you apply for Social Security. Visit www .firstgov.com to find out how to request your documents.

More things you didn't know

Why should you contribute to Social Security? I think we've covered all the reasons, but let me give you one more example of why it's important to pay into Social Security, whether you're an employee or self-employed. Years ago I interviewed a man who had been self-employed for years and years. He became disabled and tried to get benefits from Social Security. The problem was he had always claimed a loss on his self-employment, which meant he never paid Social Security taxes. And thus he wasn't eligible for any benefits. I don't know whether he really always had a loss in his business or whether he just made it look that way for tax reasons. But I've never forgotten this man, because it was so sad to see someone who desperately needed Social Security but who wasn't eligible. For this reason, I always caution people who are self-employed to pay their Social Security taxes. Protect yourself and your family!

Now for some good news. Every worker twenty-five or older automatically receives a personalized Social Security Statement annually three months before their birth month. There are a few exceptions, which you will find on the Social Security website at www.socialsecurity.gov. Your Social Security statement is mailed to the address IRS has on record for you. If you move a lot, you may not receive your statement automatically. The good news is that you can request your free Social Security statement at any time directly from Social Security.

If you've received your Social Security statement but tucked it away in a safe place and never looked at it, go pull it out to review it for accuracy. Begin by checking to ensure your name and birth date are correct. Next, review your annual earnings to ensure they are accurate. If you find errors, you'll want to correct them right away. It's much easier to get your earnings corrected now, while you still have the documentation. You'll find the instructions on the Social Security website. The Social Security statement provides an estimate of your retirement benefits at age sixty-two and full retirement age, along with survivor's and disability benefits.

One word of caution: Social Security makes assumptions based on your continuing to work at your current wage level. This means it looks at the last two years on your record. If you want a more accurate estimate, Social Security has a calculator on its website that allows you to enter your own earnings. The Social Security statement is one of the best things Social Security has ever done for the public. It's a valuable financial planning tool. I recommend you use it in conjunction with the Ballpark Estimate, an easy-to-use, two-page worksheet that helps you quickly identify approximately how much you need to save for your financial independence. Find it online at www.choosetosave.org or www.asec.org.

We've covered a lot in this chapter. You now 1) have the information and know the steps to take to prepare for unexpected emergencies and expenses, 2) know the different types of retirement accounts, and 3) know the basics about Social Security. Now it's time to learn about preparing for the other kinds of unexpected things that can happen to you and your family.

NINE

Get Prepared for the Unexpected

Protecting your financial house from potential disaster and devastation

Chapter Goals for You

- Write a will to protect your loved ones
- Prepare a durable power of attorney and advance healthcare directive
- Ensure you have the proper beneficiaries for your nonprobate assets
- Review your automobile and homeowners insurance policies for appropriate coverage
- Consider obtaining life, disability, and long-term care insurance
- Develop a disaster preparedness plan for yourself and your family

A CAUTIONARY TALE

I know it's difficult to accept our own mortality and make plans for serious illness or injury, let alone death, but preparing a will is one of the most important steps you can take to ensure your loved ones aren't left in financial chaos. My friend Kim is unfortunately a perfect example of what can happen when you don't talk about death and take the necessary actions to protect your spouse. Kim's husband, Robert, died unexpectedly seven years ago, at age sixty-one. Married eighteen years, Robert and Kim were both retired federal employees.

Robert died without a will and provided no spousal annuity for Kim, who was fifty-three at the time. Robert was receiving a retirement pension, and Kim received a disability check. When Robert retired, he didn't want to have 10 percent of his pension withheld for a spousal annuity, so he opted for the smallest percentage allowed. Instead, he bought a $250,000 life insurance policy.

So what happened when Robert died? Kim's monthly income plummeted from $6,000 to $1,200 per month! Robert didn't have a will, because he never wanted to discuss his dying. Kim was forced to hire an attorney, because one of Robert's adult sons from his first marriage decided he was entitled to a share of his father's estate.

Until Robert's death, Kim was not involved in the financial decisions. She told me in the months after Robert's death that she was in a daze. It was difficult for her to manage even ordinary tasks, and she didn't need the added frustration of trying to educate herself about financial issues.

WILL YOU OR WON'T YOU?

It is crucial for you to anticipate the unexpected now and not wait for a crisis. Kim was forced to hire an attorney and go through probate when her husband died (even though Washington is a community property state), which cost approximately $10,000. This could have easily been avoided with a will. Kim got into such a mess because her husband wouldn't talk about financial matters. As my husband, Steve, explained, "People don't want to face their mortality." He suggested that everyone read the following letter, found in *Smart Women Finish Rich,* by David Bach:

> *To those I love—*
>
> *While I understand that I have the right to determine who will inherit my property when I die, I have decided to let the courts make that decision for me, even though that might mean that people I never knew or never liked could wind up as my heirs. I also understand that there are perfectly legitimate ways of minimizing the estate taxes my loved ones will have to pay. However, because of the government's generosity to me throughout my lifetime, I have decided to let Uncle Sam take the biggest bite he can. In addition, rather than deciding who should take care of my children, I've decided that I'd rather have my family fight about it, and then let the courts just go ahead and appoint anyone they feel like.*
>
> *Finally, I know that as a result of not leaving a will, a significant portion of my assets could be eaten up by lawyer's bills, and that all of the private details of my financial affairs will be made public.*

Steve heard me read this letter at one of my forums, and it really struck a chord with him. Although we already had a will, it made him realize how important it is to have your say in what you leave behind when you die—and even if you don't want to face it, we all have an expiration date. We all remember September 11, 2001. People of all ages died that day, and dying was surely not on many of their minds as they headed out the door that morning. My guess is a lot of them didn't have a will. Although this is an extreme example, people of all ages die every day in automobile accidents. You've worked hard for your money—do you want to take a chance and let the government decide who gets your property if you die without a will?

Approximately 70 percent of Americans don't have a will, even though having a will ensures that your desires are documented.

Obviously, these numbers suggest our serious emotional resistance to admitting mortality, as though acknowledging the possibility of death will make it arrive on our doorstep all the quicker. But keep in mind that denial doesn't keep anything at bay! Take the example of a woman whose brother asked if he could name her as his life insurance beneficiary. She was appalled by the idea, as though the very act of signing the document would bring down some horrible incident, and she said absolutely not. So instead he listed a niece as his beneficiary. Just a couple of years later, the brother died in an apartment fire, leaving his sister—who had long supported her siblings from her own meager earnings, and who was struggling with serious debt—without money that she desperately could have used. As much as we don't want to think about these things, it's so important to move beyond our resistance and plan for the inevitable, sooner rather than later!

A will is a fairly simple document to create, and it protects your loved ones. It ensures your assets are given to your family or other beneficiaries, based on your wishes. Having a will is particularly important if you've been married more than once and either spouse has children from a previous marriage. If your partner is reluctant, my suggestion is to meet with an attorney by yourself. Have a draft of a will prepared, take it home, and talk about it with your husband. Explain that if he loves you, he'll review it, make any changes, and sign it, because he won't want you to suffer unnecessarily.

Most experts recommend you prepare your will with the assistance of an attorney to ensure all the details are covered. Details include designating a guardian for your minor children, and assigning an executor or personal representative. In addition to a will, you should prepare a *durable power of attorney* for financial issues, and an *advance healthcare directive* in case you are unable to handle your own medical or financial issues during your lifetime. The well-publicized case of Terri Schiavo illustrates the importance of having an advance healthcare directive, which advises your doctor, family, and friends of the types of special treatment you do or don't want at the end of your life. You can find free or low-cost legal forms online (listed in the Resources section at the back of the book). A couple of excellent online websites are www.nolo .com and www.findlegal forms.com. Both websites have a wealth of information, along with the instructions and forms you need to complete. However, before you use any legal form found online, you should have an attorney in your area review it to ensure it is valid in the courts where you live. In some instances, a living trust might be preferable to a will. Your attorney will help you determine which document is best for your situation.

Naming a guardian for your minor children and naming an executor are two important components of your will. What happens if neither parent is able to take care of the children? Without a will, the court appoints a guardian for your children, and it could easily be someone you don't want to raise your children. Before choosing a guardian, talk to the person to ensure he or she is willing to assume the responsibility. Think carefully about selecting an executor, because he or she is the person who ensures the terms of your will are carried out, oversees the distribution of your assets, and pays off any outstanding debts and taxes using the funds in your estate. Select someone who's honest, fair, patient, organized, and willing to accept the responsibility—a person who is able to work with the various personalities involved with potential heirs or beneficiaries.

Be sure to update your will if there's a change in your marital status, if you give birth to a child, or if there is any significant change in your life situation. It's particularly important to write a new will if you're in a second marriage and you have children from a former relationship. In some cases, your current spouse may automatically inherit your assets, and your children may unintentionally be left out.

Store your will in a safe place that's accessible to others. It's a good idea to provide a copy to your executor. Don't put the original will in a safe deposit box unless someone else has access to the box.

At death, some assets are called nonprobate assets, and they pass directly to the designated beneficiary (or in some cases, the joint owner). These assets include:

- Proceeds of a life insurance policy with a named beneficiary

- Money in a pension plan, individual retirement account (IRA), 401(k) or 403(b) plan, or other retirement plan with a named beneficiary

- Stocks, bonds, or U.S. Savings Bonds held in beneficiary form

- Bank accounts or investments held in joint accounts with rights of survivorship or with designated beneficiary

- Property you've transferred to a living trust

When I started working for the federal government in 1975, I remember signing lots of paperwork, some of which included designating the beneficiary for my life insurance. Many of us complete and sign similar paperwork throughout our careers. But how often do we go back and review and update our beneficiaries? When you're young and just starting out, you might designate your mother or father as your beneficiary. However, when you get married, you may want to review your life insurance policy to revise your beneficiary. If you don't take the time to update your beneficiaries and you die unexpectedly, your life insurance proceeds will not go to your spouse. Instead, your parents (or whomever you named initially) will receive the proceeds. Don't forget to periodically review your beneficiaries on the other items listed above.

· PROFIT FROM HER STORY ·

Theresa says:
Get your name on it!

Theresa's husband, Allen, died at age thirty-four, leaving Theresa to raise their young daughter alone. Allen's father was listed as the beneficiary on his IRA. Before he was married, Allen had named his father as his beneficiary back when he first started working. Allen didn't realize that the beneficiary named on his IRA would supersede the instructions in his will. This created an uncomfortable situation within the family when Allen died.

· PROFIT FROM HER STORY ·

Diane's husband says:
Thank you for sparing me the pain of the details!

My friend Diane was diagnosed with pancreatic cancer in August 2001. After getting over the shock, anger, and denial of her diagnosis, she set about putting her final wishes in order. During the next thirteen months, Diane planned her funeral service, selected the songs she wanted played, and asked a friend to sing them. Not only did she plan her funeral service, she also planned the luncheon after the service. She even hired the caterer! As you might imagine, this wasn't easy for her friends to handle, because we didn't want to think or talk about her death. However, when we attended Diane's funeral service in September 2002, it was crystal clear what an amazing gift she had given to her husband, Dean. She allowed him to deal with his grief while sparing him the pain of handling the details of her funeral arrangements.

I realize Diane's case was rather unusual, but there are plenty of other things you can do in advance to help your family during such a difficult time. One way is to write a letter with all the information they will need if you die or become incapacitated. The information should include the following.

- Full legal name, address, and phone number
- Social Security number
- Date and place of birth
- Citizenship
- Military service number and location of military service discharge papers
- Spouse's name and Social Security number
- Former spouses and dates of marriages
- Health insurance company, policy number, address, and phone number
- Primary doctor's name, address, and phone number
- Life insurance company, address, phone number, and policy number
- Attorney's name, address, and phone number
- Location of your safe deposit box, and who has the key and access
- Location of your will, and the executor's name and contact information
- Location of durable power of attorney for healthcare, and the healthcare decision maker's name and contact information
- Location of advance directive (living will)
- Location of general and durable power of attorney, and name and contact information of person designated to act on your behalf
- Organ donor information

You should also consider including your final wishes regarding funeral service and disposition of your remains. Questions to think about:

- Do you want to be cremated, buried, or entombed?

- Where do you want to be buried? What is the name and location of the cemetery?

- Do you want a funeral service? If so, do you want it to be held in a church, mortuary chapel, residence, or other location?

- Do you want a notice published in the newspaper? Which newspapers?

- Do you want people to donate to a charity in lieu of flowers? If so, what organization(s)?

- Do you want to donate your organs and tissues?

A great online resource is People's Memorial Organization, a nonprofit organization dedicated to promote planning for end-of-life decisions. Visit its website at www.peoples-memorial.org.

Believe me, I know planning for your death or a loved one's death is a difficult subject to think or talk about and follow through on, but the peace of mind it will provide both you and your loved ones makes it worth the effort. All too often, people avoid the discussion and taking any action with the belief that it won't happen to them. But I've heard way too many horror stories from women who have suffered unnecessarily because of poor estate planning by family members.

Eileen's story demonstrates how critical it is to sort out your financial lives when you marry, especially for the second time.

· PROFIT FROM HER STORY ·

Eileen says:

Don't put off getting your affairs in order!

"I met my husband, Ron, in 1993, shortly after he lost his wife to breast cancer. We got married in 1996. I had worked for sixteen years in corporate America, and I quit my job because it required a lot of travel, and Ron didn't like my being gone all the time. I took a year of retirement but got bored, and with Ron's encouragement, I started my own event-planning company, which quickly outgrew my home office. In 1999 we moved into a big, brand-new office. To soothe my fears about the big step, Ron said to me, "What are you worried about? If something happens, I'll be here to back you up."

"A week afterward, we drove from Minnesota to Colorado to spend Christmas with Ron's daughter and her family. Christmas Day we were eating dinner when Ron got up from the table, looking grayish in color, and told me he wasn't feeling well. I thought he was experiencing altitude sickness, but I immediately called 911. We were a long way from a hospital, and since it was a holiday, no cardiologist was on duty. Ron was airlifted to Denver while I made the long drive down the mountain.

"Ron died the next day, which was also my thirty-ninth birthday. We were just shy of celebrating our fourth wedding anniversary. Because Ron's first wife's battle with breast cancer had lasted twelve years, they had surpassed the cap on the amount their health insurance would pay. Ron cashed in his life insurance and other assets to pay the hospital and doctors' bills for the more than one hundred visits to the hospital they made during her last year of life.

"Before we married, Ron and I sat down and planned how we were going to pay off the medical bills. We had waited to merge

▶

our assets while Ron paid off his debts, which he had just completed before he died. We had scheduled an appointment with a financial adviser for the week after we returned from Colorado. Ron had a will, but it was outdated and didn't include me. We knew we needed a new will and had plans to do it, but we just didn't take the time to get it done.

"Even though I was very good at managing money, with my new business to run, I had turned over my finances to Ron. In hindsight, I should have been more involved with what he was doing. All of us are busy doing other things, but this is so important.

"Ron and I shared a passion for boating. When he died, I didn't know where he was storing our boat for the winter and it took me a long time to find it. And although I had never trailered or driven a larger boat, I decided I could learn. Today, I'm one of the only female captains on the river. Every year on my birthday and the anniversary of Ron's death, I give myself a gift. I'm doing my best to take a very bad situation and make something good of it. One year I went to the Amazon and another year to Burma. My advice to women is: Make sure you participate in all financial decisions, make sure the bills are getting paid, and make sure you have a will—before it's too late. I just never thought this would happen to me."

INSURANCE MAY BE DULL, BUT ONLY UNTIL YOU NEED IT

Another way to protect yourself, your loved ones, and your property is by having insurance coverage. Insurance is a contract between yourself and an insurance company. You can buy lots of different kinds of insurance, and I'm going to share some of them here to give you a starting place for checking whether you have the proper coverage. You'll find resources near the end of the chapter if you want to learn more.

Sometimes when you take out a loan, the lender requires you to have insurance coverage. For example, if you're buying your home and paying a mortgage, your lender requires you to have homeowners insurance to cover the structure of the house in case of a loss. In other words, it's protecting its property, because although your name is on the deed to the property, the lender actually owns it until you've made the last payment. The same holds true if you're buying your car on a contract—the financing company requires you to have automobile insurance. I recommend you review all your insurance policies annually and revise them as necessary.

Automobile insurance

Automobile insurance policies offer third-party liability for bodily injury and property damage, collision, comprehensive, medical payments, personal injury protection, and uninsured motorists.

- Bodily injury liability pays your legal defense costs and claims against you if your car injures or kills someone.

- Property damage liability pays your legal defense costs and claims against you if your car damages another's property. It does not cover your automobile or property.

- Medical payments or personal injury protection pays medical expenses resulting from an accident for you and others riding in your car. It will also pay for you or your family members who are injured while riding in another person's car or while walking.

- Collision pays for repairing damages to your car caused by a collision with another vehicle or other object. It doesn't matter who was responsible for the collision.

- Comprehensive physical damage pays for damages to your car resulting from theft, fire, hail, vandalism, and a number of other causes.

- Uninsured or underinsured motorist pays for costs related to injuries or property damage to you and others riding in your car caused by an uninsured, underinsured, or hit-and-run driver.

Here are some tips for reducing your automobile insurance premiums:

- Increase your deductibles. Deductibles are the amount of money you pay before your insurance kicks in. For example, if your deductible is $500 and you have a loss of $2,000, you're required to pay the first $500. Basically you're self-insuring for $500. It's crucial that you have the amount of your deducible in an emergency account, because you don't want to use your credit cards to pay the deductible. Increasing your deductible from $200 to $500 could reduce your collision and comprehensive cost by 15 to 20 percent.

- Cancel your comprehensive and/or collision coverage if you have an older car. If your car isn't worth very much, it might be in your best interest to stop paying for this coverage. But don't cancel your coverage before determining the value. You can do this through several online sources: NADA Guide—www.nadaguides.com; Kelley Blue Book—www.kbb.com; and Edmunds—www.edmunds.com.

- Comparison shop. Prices can vary greatly from company to company. A word of caution: If you've been insured with one company for a long time, you might not want to change companies for a better rate. Longevity could prevent you from being nonrenewed or canceled in case of a loss.

- Maintain a good driving record. Insurance companies consider you a higher risk for accidents if you have speeding tickets or other moving violations, or if you've had an accident in which you were responsible. In those instances, you're probably going to pay more for your insurance.

- Consider the make and model of automobile. If you have a new car, it will cost more to repair it, so your premium will be higher. Usually your premium will decrease as your car ages. Think twice before going out and buying that fancy new sports car.

- Maintain a good credit report. More and more insurance companies are using your credit report to determine your insurance risk score, which is used to determine your automobile insurance premium.

- Pay your insurance premium in one payment. Some insurance companies charge you a small fee if you make monthly installment payments. Ask your company if you get a better deal by paying your premium in one payment.

- Ask about discounts offered by your insurance company. Many insurance companies offer discounts, including ones for these situations: you have homeowners insurance with the company; you've been with the company for a long time, with a good driving record; you've taken a defensive driving course; your car is equipped with an antitheft device; your car is garaged instead of being parked on the street; you insure multiple cars; and if the young driver on your policy has a good grade point average.

Homeowners and renters insurance

Most people work hard to buy their homes and the things in it. It's crucial to insure your home and the contents in case something unforeseen happens, such as theft, fire, windstorm, or other natural disaster. If you're making a mortgage payment, your lender will require you to have property insurance, but there's more to homeowners insurance than just protecting the dwelling. You want to be sure you have enough coverage to replace your home at today's value, which is called the replacement cost.

It's essential to understand the difference between replacement cost and market value. Replacement cost is the amount needed to repair the damage or to rebuild the home to its preloss condition. For insurance purposes, the replacement cost of a home is *not* the market value of the home, its purchase price, or the outstanding amount of any mortgage loan. It does not include the value of the land, but is the cost of rebuilding your home.

Actual cash value coverage is less expensive but covers only the replacement cost minus depreciation. So if you make a claim, you won't get the full amount it costs to rebuild your home. You'll have to pay the difference out of your own pocket. Some natural disasters—such as floods, hurricanes, and earthquakes—require special coverage to be included in your policy. As events after Hurricane Katrina proved, many people did not fully understand what kind of coverage they had. If you live in areas subject to those sorts of natural disasters, it is crucial for you to sit down with your agent and make sure you fully understand which circumstances are covered and which ones are not. This could mean the difference between being able to rebuild and finding yourself suddenly homeless.

Many of us underestimate the value of our things—furniture, appliances, clothing, collections, jewelry, electronics, and so on. If you don't have a home inventory as well as appraisals for your jewelry and collections, it's time to get them. You'll find information on how to do this later in the chapter.

If you're renting, don't forget to buy renters insurance. Your landlord most likely protects the dwelling with property insurance, but unless you have renters insurance, your personal property isn't covered. That means if there is a fire and you don't have renters insurance, you will have to replace your property with your own money. Compare the cost of that with the cost of the insurance, and you'll see it's often a wise investment. That being said, it is also possible to overinsure yourself, your family, and your property, which can present its own set of financial problems, so be sure to periodically review your insurance policies and adjust them as necessary so you're well covered but aren't overextending yourself.

Vicki's cautionary tale shows how even careful preparedness can't keep you safe from everything—but insurance sure helps.

> ### · PROFIT FROM HER STORY ·
>
> *Vicki* says:
>
> Along with insurance, sometimes you also need luck!
>
> "What would you do if your house went up in flames? This question skipped through my thoughts when I was a surgical resident in the Harborview Burn Center. While participating in the care of burn patients under the direction of world-class doctors, I learned what fire does to bodies. Then I got to learn from personal experience what fire does to lives.
>
> "A malfunction in my dryer led to a fire that quickly consumed my old wooden attic. What contents of mine didn't burn were enveloped in smoke and soot. My charred and melted car, parked a few yards away, demonstrated the power of the heat. I'm thankful I escaped unharmed.
>
> "Ironically, I thought I'd done everything right to prevent a house fire, and in fact, I had. I got routine maintenance on my boiler that included cleaning of my dryer vents. I had smoke alarms, a carbon monoxide detector, and fire extinguishers. Yet a simple malfunctioning switch in the dryer changed my life in a heartbeat.
>
> "I was, however, able to see many blessings in the event. I could have put the clothes in the dryer and gone to sleep as I do so many times, most likely resulting in my own death. My son was not in the house at the time of the fire. I'm not a patient in the burn unit. Sure, I lost many things that were dear, but some precious items, such as my son's baby book, survived.
>
> "I also feel blessed by the police and fire professionals who managed the fire and looked after me and my pets. After I dropped
>
> ▶

▶

off my dog with family and returned to my charred house, the firefighters placed my elderly cat in my arms. They found her hiding in the closet and had given her oxygen. When I said she seemed disoriented, the fire marshal took us to the emergency vet clinic. After a sleepless night, I returned to my house in borrowed clothes, and the firefighter who stayed at the house all night helped me scoop my dying goldfish to clean water.

"The other big blessing was that I had chosen a good insurance company and had excellent coverage. My take-charge claims adjuster assembled an extraordinary team to help me rebuild my life. I'm also lucky to be part of a compassionate community. I left my burning house shoeless on the rainy night of the fire, and shoes, a coat, and a leash for my dog magically appeared from caring neighbors. I have been the recipient of untold acts of kindness, big and small, that have touched my heart.

"So what do you do when your house goes up in flames? I recognize the inherent vulnerability of life and mourn many losses, yet I celebrate my many blessings. I observe that the very best in people comes out at the very worst of times. I experience the power of a community to support healing from a life-altering event such as this. I remind myself that the most important thing in life, the caring connections with others, cannot be consumed in flames."

· PROFIT FROM HER STORY ·

Kim says:
Be sure you understand everything about your home!

"I soon realized the importance of taking notes on your finances, taxes, cars, and household maintenance (heater, air conditioner,

▶

water turnoff valve, etc.). Every little thing that happens after your husband dies is monumental, and it's scary. I established a list of services and companies. Whenever a service person came to the house, I took notes. I could have avoided the cost of hiring service people, I could have saved money, and it wouldn't have been so frightening if I'd learned about these things when Robert was alive.

"My husband had a financial adviser, and Robert had told me if anything ever happened to him, 'You can trust this guy; just call him up.' So I did trust him, but unfortunately, he *wasn't* trustworthy. One week after Robert died, the financial adviser had me sign a document giving him the authority to invest my money as he saw fit, though I told him I wanted to preserve my capital. But because I was emotionally paralyzed, I lost about $100,000 in a year.

"Finally I took the advice of someone I knew I could trust, and I called several financial advisers and interviewed them. Then I moved my investments to another company, and I'm now working with a financial adviser who takes the time to answer my questions. Please beware that there are so-called financial advisers out there who prey on people who are vulnerable.

"Today I'm financially stable for a couple of reasons. I had to sell my home with its $1,700 monthly mortgage, and I bought a condo with an $800 monthly mortgage. However, I quickly realized I didn't like condo living, so I sold it for a profit and bought another house with a $500 monthly mortgage.

"My best advice is to prepare for a guaranteed monthly income that covers your basic expenses."

Spousal annuity

One option is to choose the survivor's annuity offered on your husband's retirement benefits. Although his monthly retirement check will be reduced to cover this benefit, it's an excellent way to ensure you have a regular monthly cash flow for the rest of your life if you outlive him. Buying life insurance is another and possibly a less expensive option, but I encourage you to review your options in detail and talk with a financial adviser before making a decision. Federal survivor annuity benefits include healthcare benefits. If your spouse doesn't select the survivor annuity, you will not have healthcare coverage under his benefits when he dies.

Life insurance

Life insurance protects your loved ones, the people you leave behind when you die. It can provide people who depend on you financially an ongoing income to replace your income, or it can be paid in one lump sum. Life insurance can also provide money to cover your outstanding debts and funeral expenses. On the other hand, some people don't need life insurance and probably shouldn't spend their hard-earned money on it. For example, if you're single with no dependents, then you probably don't need life insurance.

Life insurance is of two basic types—term and cash value coverage. Term insurance is relatively inexpensive. You pay an annual premium to provide your beneficiaries with coverage in case of your death. The policy has no value while you are alive. If you cancel the policy or stop making payments, the policy has no value at all. Cash value insurance is not only an insurance policy, but it also includes other financial products, such as a savings or investment account. The premium you pay is much higher than a term policy. Much of the cost is incurred during the early years of the policy. Your savings or cash surrender value grows the longer you have the insurance, and you can borrow against the cash value in your policy. If you decided to buy a cash value life insurance policy, your goal should be to keep it for life. Why? Because it's so expensive in the early years and grows in value the longer you have it.

Long-term care insurance

Many people think of long-term care insurance just as something old people need. But in reality, it's for people of all ages. Long-term care insurance provides assistance for a person who needs help with her physical or emotional needs for an extended period. It helps people with an illness, injury, disability, or terminal condition. Another myth is that Medicare will provide indefinite coverage if you're in a skilled nursing home. Medicare covers only up to one hundred days, and you'll be required to pay a share of your care beginning with the twenty-first day. You'll find more detailed information on the Medicare website, at www.medicare.gov. If you're fortunate enough to have health insurance coverage, it probably won't cover assistance that you might need for an extended period. If you're not sure, get out your health insurance policy and review the coverage. If you can't find the answer, call your insurance company and ask.

The following story of a couple in their forties illustrates the potential value of having this insurance long before you *think* you'll need it.

· PROFIT FROM HER STORY ·

Carol and *Randy* say:
Just when you least expect it . . . !

"My husband, Randy, is a State Farm Insurance agent in Boise, Idaho. I worked with him and talked with people daily about the importance of planning for their futures by protecting their assets and liabilities. In 2002, we qualified for a trip to Maui that the company was offering. Randy got his scuba certification so he could go diving with friends while we were in Maui. The evening before we left, we went to our daughter's softball game, sitting in the rain and blowing wind, dreaming of the warm days ahead on the beaches of Maui. We arranged for Randy's sister to come and stay with our four children, and we were so excited about a week on our own in Maui. When we arrived, we spent the day playing in the calm waves and enjoying the warmth of the sun.

"On the third day, Randy surprised me with a semiprivate snorkeling trip to celebrate our twenty-second anniversary. We saw sea turtles, beautiful fish, and coral, and we even spotted whales. Dolphins swam alongside our boat. We were served a delicious lunch aboard the boat and had time to relax and enjoy each other. It was paradise.

"We had hoped to hook up with friends so Randy could go out on that long-awaited first scuba dive, but we couldn't find them. Hating to waste the remainder of the day, we decided to take our boogie boards to a beach, where the waves were rumored to be bigger and better for boogie boarding. As we approached the beach, we could see people scattered in the water waiting for just the right wave.

"Our first clue that the beach was dangerous should have been that most people were farther out in the water than is usual. We

▶

▶

should have paid more attention to the numerous sandbars we could see when we got into the water. As we waded about knee-deep in the turbulent water, I really was uncomfortable getting in, but Randy, being the daring one, plowed his way into the water. He had gone about twenty yards from me and could see a wave approaching quickly. As I watched, he turned his board to catch a three-foot wave, which carried him up on the top and broke very quickly. I could see his feet tumbling in the water. I watched for him to resurface and shake himself off after the tumble, but he didn't show up.

"After several seconds, the boogie board that was attached to his wrist came up, with Randy floating facedown in the water. I screamed for help and ran into the water to grab his arm so the water would not carry him farther out. As I held him, I was over-taken by another wave and dragged under water.

"By the time I resurfaced, several people had come to my aid. Six to eight people assisted in dragging Randy's limp body to the beach. Fortunately, in the crowd were a retired physician and his firefighter grandson. They quickly organized people to start CPR. I can remember thinking, *This can't be happening to us.*

"As the CPR continued, my one and only job was to pray for his life. I yelled at him that I needed him and that he couldn't leave. It was an hour before an ambulance got us to a hospital. During this agonizing ride, I continued to think over and over again, *This can't be happening to us.*

"Randy was quickly sedated, put on a ventilator, and taken into x-ray. The doctors determined that the force of the wave had driven his head into one of the sandbars. He had a broken neck, and there was considerable damage to his spinal cord. The doctors didn't really talk in language I could comprehend. I think it's because they didn't want me to know how badly Randy was

▶

injured. What this really meant was that my husband, my eternal companion, was paralyzed, and if he survived his injury, he might not ever walk or breathe on his own again.

"I hadn't called home, because I didn't really know what I was going to tell anyone. I was still thinking, *This can't be happening to us.* When I finally called my sister-in-law about Randy's accident, I could feel the presence of my children watching her as they came to understand that something unexpected had happened. All I could do was tell them that everything would be okay, which was a pretty big promise to make.

"I spent my days and nights next to Randy as he drifted in and out of consciousness. His mouth was filled with tubes, he was hooked up to machines, and the hiss of the ventilator was our constant companion. The break in his neck at the C3 level made it questionable if he would be able to regain the use of his diaphragm. After ten days, we returned to Boise via air ambulance. After a second surgery, Randy was moved to Craig Rehabilitation Hospital in Denver.

"During his stay there, my life consisted of traveling back and forth between Denver and Boise, keeping our children organized and preparing them for the road ahead, as well as keeping our business up and running. Randy and I began to accept the harsh reality of our future. Finally, six months after leaving for our trip to Maui, Randy arrived home in a power wheelchair that he operates with his mouth though a sip and puff straw.

"There is no such thing as an easy day at our house. Randy requires assistance 24 hours a day, 7 days a week, 365 days a year. Absolutely all of his needs must be met by someone else. Overwhelming doesn't begin to cover it. Plus, I still have four children to care for, bills to pay, and a house and a business to run.

"Several months before we went to Maui, we had met with an attorney to get our wills and medical directives in order. It was a difficult appointment to keep, but it gave us both great peace of mind once it was done. We had made a habit of reviewing our own insurance policies at least once a year to consider possible needs we might have in the future. Amazingly, just six months before Randy's accident, we had bought long-term care insurance—one of the wisest decisions we've ever made.

"Having long-term care insurance has given me choices. Because of this protection, I am able to have someone assist me with his care. I am able to be a mother to my children. I am able to continue to live a small piece of my own life. The benefits of Randy's policy will pay up to $75,000 per year for his care. There is no way I could have come up with this kind of money. I would have had no choice but to do it *all* on my own or go completely into debt. I thank God every day that we had the foresight to get started early with needs such as this. If nothing else, I am able to have piece of mind, which is priceless.

"Randy and I are moving forward with life. He chose to continue to work as a State Farm agent, and he thinks he owes it to others to make sure they really understand how important it is to be prepared for any eventualities. His outlook on life now is very different. We're both adapting to all the changes we've had to make in our lives, but we are moving forward."

Disability insurance

According to the Social Security Administration, almost three in ten of today's twenty-year-olds will become disabled before reaching age sixty-seven—a staggering 30 percent! And 70 percent of the private sector workforce has no long-term disability insurance. Disability insurance ensures your power to earn money, which to most people is their most valuable financial asset. Just think about it: You're working around the house, stumble down the stairs, and break your leg. You miss work because you need surgery, recovery time, and physical therapy. You're divorced with two children and have no money in savings and no disability insurance. What do you do?

Disability insurance is often overlooked, partly because it just seems like one more bill to pay every month. You're young, or at least too young to become disabled, right? Wrong! Most of us don't think that bad things happen to good people, but you've already read stories that prove otherwise. Disability insurance can be expensive, but the bottom line is, if you're out of work and not getting a paycheck, you need a source of income to pay your bills. Disability insurance pays you a monthly income if you're unable to work because of an accident or illness.

Social Security has a disability benefit, but it's for people who have worked long enough to be eligible (length of time worked depends on your age), have a disability that has lasted or is expected to last twelve months or longer, or is expected to result in death. In addition, there is a five-month waiting period. It's not designed for people who are unable to work for a short time.

Resources for comparison shopping

Insure.com
www.insure.com

Insurance.com
www.insurance.com

Bankrate.com
www.bankrate.com

Insurance Information Institute
www.iii.org

National Association of Insurance Commissioners
www.naic.org

GETTING PREPARED FOR NATURAL DISASTERS

That's the thing about Mother Nature—you never know when she'll vent her wrath in your direction. When it does happen to you, you'll be in a hurry to leave your home, in shock, and you'll probably not be thinking straight. It's so much better to take the time now to get yourself and your family prepared. Hurricane Katrina is a *big* reminder why it's important to be prepared for all types of disasters, including additional ones that can follow in the aftermath of natural catastrophe, such as theft, water damage, or fire.

Think it won't happen to you? I was surprised when I added up how many different kinds of disasters I'd experienced in some way during the past twenty years. I lived in the San Francisco Bay Area during the big earthquake in 1989; I was working on the thirtieth floor of a building in downtown Seattle in 2001 when we had our big earthquake there; in 2002 I was home alone when a fire broke out in our house; and the same year, I was in Fort Lauderdale, preparing to go on a cruise with a friend, when we were evacuated to a Red Cross shelter to await Hurricane Jeanne. You can't ever know when disaster will strike, so no matter how lucky you think you are or how much of a gambler you are, it's always better to be prepared.

Begin with a plan. Sit down with your family and talk about why it's important to be prepared for disasters. Working together and sharing responsibilities is a great way to get everyone involved. Talk about the types of disasters that might happen where you live. For example, here in western Washington, we experience lots of power outages and snow and ice during the winter, and we also had a major earthquake several years ago.

Determine a place for your family to meet if you have an emergency at home. For example, we had a laundry room fire one night when I was home alone with our two dogs and cat. I woke to the sound of the smoke alarm and tried to get into the laundry room but couldn't because of the fumes. I called 911, grabbed my pets, put them in my car, and drove it away from the house to a safe place. I waited for the fire department to arrive, and it showed up several minutes later but didn't come into our driveway because our address was not clearly marked. We live in a rural area, up a gravel driveway with two homes on it. It had never occurred to us that we should have our address clearly marked outside our house, as well as on our mailbox.

You also need to plan a second meeting place outside your neighborhood in case you're unable to return home. Provide the address and phone number to everyone in your household. Make arrangements for an out-of-state contact to be your family contact person. After a major disaster, it's usually easier to call out of state, because the in-state phone lines are jammed. Make contact cards with the information, and keep one in your wallet. You'll find an emergency contact card on the American Red Cross website at www.redcross.org. It's great to develop a plan, but the second part is carrying it out! Post-Katrina, many towns have stepped up their emergency preparedness, with information and materials available, as well as classes you can take to become thoroughly ready for anything.

· PROFIT FROM HER STORY ·

Nancy says:
Preparedness is in the details!

"I was away in Baltimore in 2001 when we had the Seattle earthquake. My son was in the Boy Scouts, and one of his projects had

►

> ► been to prepare the family for emergencies. We had an emergency plan and an out-of-state contact, but I'm the only one in the family who remembered. I spent many frustrating hours worrying about the safety of my husband and kids."

Be sure to post emergency telephone numbers by your phones and teach your children how to dial 911 in an emergency. All family members should also know how to turn off the sources of natural gas, electricity, and water. Take time to teach everyone how to use a fire extinguisher, and make sure you have working smoke detectors in your home. It's so heartbreaking when you hear about families who have died because they either did not have a smoke detector or it wasn't working. We always hated our kitchen smoke detector because it's so sensitive that it goes off whenever we burn toast, but I was so thankful for that sensitive smoke detector when we had the fire in our laundry room!

You should also install carbon monoxide detectors in your home. Tragically, quite a few people died of carbon monoxide poisoning in my area in a recent winter by misusing electrical generators in their homes and apartments during power outages.

Another must is having a disaster-supplies kit, but I also think it's one of the toughest things to put together, because it contains so many things. The Red Cross recommends six basics you should stock in your disaster-supply kit in case of an emergency: water, food, first aid supplies, clothing and bedding, tools, and emergency supplies, plus special items for medical conditions. You should review your supply kit periodically to make sure the food and water are still usable. Visit the Red Cross website at www.redcross.org for a detailed list of what should be included in a disaster-supply kit.

Whatever you do, be sure to get an evacuation box to protect your financial paperwork. It should be fireproof, lockable, and light enough to carry. Put inside a copy of the inventory of your assets, liabilities, and income. Include photocopies of your driver's license, Social Security card, birth certificate, marriage certificate, passports, will, insurance policies, and home and automobile titles. You'll also want to keep in it some cash or travelers checks, and extra regular checks. Another idea is to scan this information onto a disk or a portable drive. Keep one copy of the disk in your evacuation box, a copy in your safe deposit box, and send a copy to a trusted family member or friend who lives in a different area. Above all, keep the box where it's easy to grab on the way out the door, such as on a shelf in a hall closet, and make sure every family member knows where it is. Conduct family emergency drills regularly, which is especially critical if you have young children and/or live in a rural area far from emergency services.

Having an up-to-date household inventory is essential. Yes, I know this is a big job, but it's also a necessary task. Begin by taking pictures or videotaping your home. Walk through the rooms in your home, describing the contents as you go. Open cupboards, closets, and drawers to show the contents. If you're videotaping, name each item—and if you're really organized, give the model and serial number. Numerous computer software programs for taking a home inventory are available. The Insurance Information Institute (www.knowyourstuff.org) has a free program that lets you catalog every room in your house along with photos. It also allows to you to list each item and include a photo, make, model, serial number, date and place purchased, and description. Another solution if you're just not up to the doing your own home inventory is to hire someone to do it. Some members of the National Association of Professional Organizers provide home inventory services. Visit its website at www.napo.net.

I hope this information clears up some of the mysteries about preparing for your future—and inspires you to get on with it! If you're still feeling daunted by it all, fear not—help is just around the corner of the next chapter.

TEN

Get Sound Professional Advice, Support, and Help

You don't have to do it alone—how to find the assistance you need

Chapter Goals for You

- Identify aspects of your finances where you have questions or concerns
- Research financial professionals you might want to consult
- Interview several advisers before picking one
- Determine if there are other types of advisers you could profit from consulting

COACHES AREN'T JUST FOR SPORTS—OR KIDS!

Throughout this book, you've been provided places to write your goals and action plans. I haven't yet discussed securing professional advice to help you succeed in your journey. Just as you need to find reliable plumbers and repair people to keep your house in good shape, you need to do something similar with your financial house. It's crucial to surround yourself with support: friends, support groups, financial advisers and other professionals, coaches, and so on. Don't try to go it alone.

For example, a professional organizer can help you sort through your financial records and get them and your office in order. A personal coach can motivate you to determine your financial values, goals, and what's important to you. Even if you live in a remote area, coaching is available by phone and online.

Although it's not absolutely necessary to consult one, a good financial adviser can also be your coach and mentor. She can assist you in identifying your problem areas, develop strategies to help you reach your financial goals, assist you in setting priorities, save you time by researching investments, and help you make money with your investments.

HOW TO FIND A QUALIFIED FINANCIAL ADVISER

To begin the process of finding a good financial adviser, obtain the names of three candidates. Ask friends and colleagues for referrals. If possible, interview all three financial advisers before determining which one best fits your needs. Below are some questions to ask when you conduct your interviews.

- Can you tell me about your work, educational experience, and how long you have been in business? (Though there is no right or wrong answer to that question.)

- How are you paid for your services? A financial adviser can be paid for her services in several ways. One method is fee-based services, which is based on total assets being managed. Another method is commission only, which is when you pay a commission each time you buy or sell an investment. You need to determine which fee structure best fits your needs.

- How often do you or someone from your office communicate with your clients? Your financial adviser can be your financial coach; therefore you want to communicate with her at least twice a year to ensure that you keep in touch with your investments. Your relationship with your financial adviser is important in achieving and maintaining financial fitness.

Remember that it's up to you to know how your investments are being managed—don't rely solely on your financial adviser without taking responsibility for overseeing your investments.

- Can you provide references of clients with needs similar to mine? Talking with other clients can be very valuable. Ask them if they are happy with the service the financial adviser provides. You might also want to ask them if the financial adviser has any strengths and/or weaknesses.

Remember, though some of these questions may sound a bit intimidating to ask, *you* are the one in charge. *You* are the one doing the hiring of someone to help manage *your* money. Take whatever steps necessary to ensure your comfort in working with these advisers. One trick is to ask these questions over the phone when you are screening candidates. That way, when you sit down face-to-face, the potentially uncomfortable questions have already been answered. While you may not want to spend the money to pay a financial adviser, getting the advice of an expert is definitely worthwhile. She'll help you make good investment decisions to ensure you're financially secure.

· PROFIT FROM HER STORY ·

Kathy says:
Don't wait—ask for advice sooner rather than later!

"I thought only *rich* people had a financial adviser, but now I see that if you desire to *be* rich and aren't, you need a financial adviser! I've found a great financial adviser and wish I had sought her direction years ago. She is helping me in more ways than I

▶

▶

had imagined. We've set up my bills to be paid automatically online, and I've started funding my financial freedom account. My financial adviser is helping me on the pathway to freedom from money concerns."

So what's a certified financial planner (CFP)?

Financial advisers are individuals who provide financial advice, services, or products for compensation. This category includes a wide range of financial professionals, including financial planners, registered representatives, money managers, and investment advisers.

Some financial professionals have earned the title of certified financial planner. These individuals have completed education, examination, and experience requirements determined by the Certified Financial Planner's Board. Check out www.cfp.net for a list of questions to ask when interviewing a potential financial adviser or certified financial planner.

· PROFIT FROM HER STORY ·

Cynthia says:
It's important to be involved!

"While I'm learning more every day, I still feel a little unsure about the whole thing, and I want to be involved, not just let someone else handle things for me. I need to fund my own retirement, since I have never worked full time, so I have recently invested in mutual funds and have contributed to my IRA for this year. After meeting with a Charles Schwab representative, I now have a diversified

▶

> portfolio! It was painless, and now I should have a nice little nest egg for my retirement. I still have some work to do and will keep on top of my investments and review them in six months. It's really quite a job, and now I know why we pay others for advice."

You may also want to contact the organizations listed below to verify the financial adviser's credentials:

Certified Financial Planner Board of Standards
www.cfp-board.org

Financial Industry Regulatory Authority
www.finra.org

North American Securities Administrators Association
www.nasaa.org

National Association of Insurance Commissioners
www.naic.org

STILL OTHER KINDS OF PROFESSIONAL HELP

Other financial professionals you may need to consult include bankers, mortgage brokers, insurance agents, and Realtors. How do you determine which professional is the best one to work with? It may take some investigative work on your part, but it will probably pay off in the long run. Start by asking people you know for names of advisers they trust and work with. You may want to meet with a couple of financial professionals before determining who fits best with your goals. I recommend looking for someone who has integrity and is trustworthy, honest, and enthusiastic about working with you. The bottom line is this: Make sure you feel comfortable with the person.

Choosing a bank

Your banking relationship is an important decision. Don't just pick the one that hands out dog biscuits at the drive-through window! A good way to get to know a bank is by checking out its website. You'll be able to research company history and financials, products, and services, and compare current product rates. You can learn a lot about the company before visiting the local branch. Although banks offer similar products and services, here are several points to consider when choosing a bank that will be a good financial fit for you.

- Large national banks versus small community banks. Consider a bank that is convenient for your daily activities. You'll need easy access to your bank from work or home. If your work requires you to travel, you may want to consider a large national bank that has a branch and ATM network that provides access while you're on the road. If you travel infrequently, a community bank may be the best fit. Community banks offer the same competitive products and rates as the big national banks, but because decisions are made locally, you may have access to more personalized service. For instance, some community banks have forgone the automated phone system for a real person on the phone lines—very helpful when you need personal attention.

- Online banking and bill pay. One of the most convenient ways to bank is online. You can pay bills, transfer funds between accounts, and view canceled checks and statements online. Most banks have an online banking demonstration on their websites for you to try.

- Rates and product offers. Consider the types of products you'll want from your bank. Beyond a checking account, you may want to research rates and product information on credit cards, savings accounts, loans, mortgages, and certificates of deposit. Most banks even offer a full line of investment products, such as IRAs and mutual funds. Just make sure you understand all the fees involved. Read the fine print. Even though some banks claim to offer free checking, there may be hidden charges. When opening a checking account, banks are required to provide a Truth in Savings Disclosure. This document, although lengthy, should describe all fees and rate information. If you plan to have more than one account, look for banks that offer special discounts or added features, because some banks consider your combined balances and provide special discounts or services.

- Customer service. Think about what's most important to you in a banking relationship. Is it important to develop a long-term, personal relationship with bank staff? It's a good idea to visit the branch where you would conduct most of your business and observe the staff. Are the tellers friendly and knowledgeable? Is the manager or customer service staff accessible? Are the banking hours convenient for you? For instance, is the bank open on Saturdays? If you've been with your bank for a long time, but it's not providing you the things that are important to you, consider moving your account(s) to another bank. In today's economy, banks are offering lots of perks to attract new customers.

- Friends' and family's recommendations. Your friends or family may be able to provide good examples of their banking experiences. Testimonials are one of the best ways to choose any service or product.

Ten questions to ask a mortgage company

As with other financial decisions, when choosing a mortgage company, you have various options. Don't just pick the one across the street from your office. It always pays to do your homework. The top ten questions to ask:

1. What is the average number of days it takes for you to issue a firm loan approval?

2. Are the rates you are quoting today good thirty days from now?

3. If we are locked in and rates go up, what is your policy if our rate lock expires?

4. What are the total fees associated with our loan?

5. How will this loan affect my financial goals?

6. Are you closing at least one hundred loans a year, and/or how long have you been in the business?

7. Can I be preapproved before buying the property?

8. What is the annual percentage rate (APR) on this program?

9. What percentage of the loans you take actually close?

10. Can you provide me with the names of five past customers I can contact?

· PROFIT FROM HER STORY ·

Kristen says:
Financial professionals can find
creative ways to free up your money!

"I met with my new mortgage broker, and she is working on some scenarios with my investment properties and residence to restructure the financing to create cash flow and free up some of my money. This will allow me to buy some additional investment property and provide me with additional monthly income."

Don't limit seeking advice to typical scenarios. For instance, you can still profit from the advice of a mortgage broker even after you've refinanced your property. Of course, seeking input ahead of time is even better!

> **· PROFIT FROM HER STORY ·**
>
> *Beth* says:
> **A mortgage broker can help fix your mistakes!**
>
> "I met with my mortgage broker this past Saturday at her office. I recently refinanced my home and realized even in my financial ignorance that the deal wasn't that great. I needed someone to examine this new mortgage with me and advise me about where I am and where I should go. My broker took that time, listened to my financial tale of woe, and gave me a path to follow. I was so impressed with her knowledge and positive outlook."

How to pick an insurance company

Whether you're a first-time buyer of insurance, new to a community, or already have insurance but are looking for a better deal, you should be asking several questions.

- Is the company from which you are buying well known? What is its reputation?

- Does the company operate as a direct insurer or through a local agent?

- Does the company offer all the insurance products and services you need, or will you need to work with multiple insurance companies? Most insurance companies offer a discount if all your auto, homeowners, and other property insurance policies are with them.

- If you choose a company that operates with an agency system (an agent who sells insurance for numerous companies), is the agent from whom you're buying a visible, established member of your community—someone you know and trust?

- What about price? Because there are hundreds of companies competing for your business, prices vary—sometimes a lot. It may pay to shop around. Be sure the premiums you're quoted are for equal amounts of coverage. And don't forget to ask about any discounts for which you might qualify.

- How about service? Price is important, but saving money won't mean much unless you get the service you need—when and how you need it. What options are available for paying your premium or reporting claims? How will your claim be handled?

- How about solvency? Is the company you're considering still going to be in business when you file your claim? Your state Department of Insurance has financial rating information on all companies that do business in its state.

Once you've decided on a company and an agent, there are more questions to ask.

- How much coverage do you need? Consider your needs in light of your assets and income. How much can you afford to pay if there's a big judgment against you because of an accident? How much will it take to rebuild your home and replace your belongings in case of a fire?

- What about deductibles? Deductibles lower your premiums— but they also increase the amount of loss that comes out of your pocket. How much additional risk are you willing to take in order to save? Consider whether the savings are enough to offset the risk of footing the entire cost of your loss.

- Insurance is not a generic commodity. It is a product that should be tailored to each individual. Make sure you find a company and local agent to fit your needs.

Here are some shopping tips:

- Talk to people you trust and ask for recommendations, and contact independent sources such as your state's Department of Insurance.

- Ask about discounts! What appears to be a higher rate may actually be in the ballpark if you qualify for discounts.

- Look for a company that is available how and when you want service: on the phone, in person, or online.

How to select a real estate agent or broker

Since buying or selling a home can be one of the most important financial processes in your life, it's important to select the right agent. The process can and usually does produce a moderate to high level of stress.

Before we begin, let's talk about the difference between a real estate broker and a real estate agent. Each state regulates both brokers and agents. Brokers have more training, education, and experience, while agents are usually required to meet minimum levels of education, training, and testing. Before you hire a real estate professional, you should interview at least three different people. Start by getting recommendations from friends, coworkers, family, neighbors, and others you trust who have recently used that professional and had a good experience. Then search the Internet, home magazines, and local newspapers to see the kinds of marketing that various real estate companies are doing in your area. During the interview, explain your needs, including how you like to work and what you expect. Below is a list of questions to ask:

- How long have you been in real estate sales? While experience is not a guarantee of skill, years of experience can be an asset. The counterbalance with a less-experienced professional might be her level of enthusiasm and willingness to work with you. No matter how long she's been in real estate, what you're looking for is her full-time commitment.

- Are you a full-time real estate professional? Is this her career or is it something she's filling in her time with until she can work full time at her real job? A full-time real estate professional may have more time to devote to you.

- What designations do you hold? This is the alphabet soup that appears on real estate professionals' business cards: certified residential specialist (CRS), graduate Realtor Institute (GRI), accredited buyer's Realtor (ABR), and many more. These designations require real estate professionals to complete specialized real estate training. Although credentials alone don't always guarantee a professional's expertise, it does indicate a certain level of professional commitment.

- What's your business philosophy? Although there's no right answer to this question, the response will help you determine what's important to the real estate professional. Is she interested in fast sales, service, and so on? It will also help you determine how closely her goals and business emphasis are matched to your own goals.

- How many homes did you and your company sell last year? How many days did it take you to sell the average home? How does that compare to the overall market? Obviously you're looking for a professional who has a good track record.

- What types of marketing approaches will you use to sell my home? You're looking for a professional who is aggressive, with innovative approaches to marketing your property. Find out how quickly your listing will be up on the multiple listing service (MLS), in which newspaper(s) your property will be advertised and how often, how your property will be promoted to other professionals, when your property will be on the broker's tour, and when and how often your professional will be holding an open house.

- Will you be representing me exclusively, or will you act as a dual agent for both the buyer and seller? Dual representation comes with inherent conflict of interest as the professional attempts to fairly represent two opposing clients and collect her full commission. A good professional will explain the agency relationship to you and describe the rights of each party.

- How will you keep me informed of the progress of my transaction? The answer to this question depends on your desires. Do you want to be updated once a week or contacted only if there's a hot prospect? Do you prefer to be contacted by phone or email? Communication with your agent is critical to ensure a smooth transaction.

- What are your fees or commissions?

- Can you give me the names and phone numbers of your three most recent clients?

You might ask many other questions, but this is a good start. The important thing is to determine whether the agent is someone with whom you have genuine rapport, and if she is someone you think has the expertise, enthusiasm, and energy to help you achieve your goals.

Now, don't you feel better knowing so much great help is out there? There's just one final step to getting your financial house in perfect order. And it's the easiest and most fulfilling one of all.

· ELEVEN ·

Share Your Wealth of Knowledge

Savoring the results of your hard work and inspiring others

Chapter Goals for You

- Determine your net worth
- Complete the final checklist
- Make your final action plan
- Find ways to share your knowledge

YOU BUILT THIS HOUSE ON SOLID GROUND

If you've been diligent about using the information in this book, you'll be well on your way to getting your financial house in tip-top shape. I hope you can see now that breaking down this massive undertaking into manageable chunks makes it attainable, even for those of you who balk at big projects. So congratulations for your perseverance in doing this life-altering work!

For some encouragement, read how Sherry feels after doing some of the work in this book.

· PROFIT FROM HER STORY ·

Sherry says:
The net result of many small steps is big change!

"I have completed several of my action steps, and I am feeling relief and a sense of accomplishment and security now. Challenges are cutting back on frivolous spending. That's the biggie. Tracking my spending wasn't pleasant (I knew it wouldn't be), but it helped me to get a plan in place, and I am now conscious of where my money is going. I have met with an investment counselor and opened a Roth IRA and mutual fund with automatic monthly payments to each! I switched my retirement account to be self-directed rather than having someone else decide where to invest. And I also got my fifteen-year-old son involved by opening an investment account for him too! I have committed to paying an extra $100 each month to my credit card account *and* committed $200 to a savings account each month. These are *big* changes for me, and I'm feeling empowered once again."

Sometimes you get inspired—by reading a book such as this, for example—but then the weeks go by, life intervenes, and you revert to your former ways. Alisa had that experience, but she was determined to keep her dream of financial stability alive, so she really went the extra miles to get it done. If you feel your resolve weakening, reread her story, and don't give up!

· PROFIT FROM HER STORY ·

Alisa says:

Never give up, even when your motivation gets sluggish!

"In early 2006, I was forty-seven years old, going through a divorce, and reexamining my life. I had decided that financially I was not where I thought I should be or wanted to be in my life. At the rate I was going, I would never be able to retire, much less at fifty-five or sixty. I had a well-paying, secure profession but realized I hadn't managed my money wisely. I knew what I wanted and should do; I just didn't know how to go about it. I did not have financial role models.

"My sister, who lives in Washington, told me about an upcoming MoneyWi$e Women Forum here in Boise, so I rather skeptically signed up. Even the day of the seminar, I was talking myself out of going. Well, I went, and *oh, my gosh!* I was like a sponge, just absorbing all the information I could. I was on the edge of my seat throughout the day as I listened to so many dynamic people who were willing to help women reach their financial goals. I looked around the room and talked to other women attending the seminar, and I realized that there were many women who were in a similar financial situation.

"Afterward I was very motivated. I went home and started reading all the suggested books and started getting my financial house in order. I made one-year, two-year, and five-year goals for myself, but after a few weeks I found myself running out of momentum. I didn't have the support here in Boise to keep me motivated and to discuss issues. So I contacted my sister in Washington and told her of my plans to join her at a forum in Tacoma. With my sister and her friends, we managed to attend all the breakout sessions and share the information we obtained with each other. Once again, I was motivated and made many new contacts.

▶

"But a few months later, I felt my motivation decreasing again. We discussed the possibility of a book club here in Boise for all the women who had attended the Boise seminar, and now we have an active book club. We not only read the books; we follow the recommendations in the books. We recently bought the Cashflow game and will start having regular game nights.

"I refinanced my house using a dynamic new loan and should be able to pay off my house a lot faster than with the loan I had previously. I have also traveled to Washington to attend investment seminars and will be investing in real estate in the near future.

"It has been nearly a year since I attended the seminar in Boise. As a direct result, I have gotten my financial house in order. I have attended several financial and investment seminars, I monitor my credit report, I started a financial book club, and I meet monthly with this dynamic, motivated group of women. My financial knowledge has grown immensely in the past year, and I am on the track to financial freedom."

Also keep in mind that it's important to start this process regardless of your age or circumstances. Virginia got a late start, but she's already encouraged by her progress.

· PROFIT FROM HER STORY ·

Virginia says:
Don't wait another day!

"I am fifty-three years old, recently divorced, and in the process of rewriting every aspect of my life. The financial planning aspect

> ▶
>
> of this process is tremendously time consuming, but it is probably the highest and best use of my time right now. I would have to say that the most difficult piece (especially at my age) is the necessity to completely reinvent one's present and future financial life. It is most unsteadying, while at the same time it is life affirming that it can be done, and it can be done well."

HOW TO KNOW WHAT YOU'RE WORTH

Of course, I'm talking financially, but one result of putting all this effort into your education will undoubtedly be a rise in your sense of self-worth. But your net worth statement is a snapshot of where you stand financially. It's an important tool to analyze your financial progress. It's also a useful guide to help you establish your financial goals and manage your money to achieve your goals.

The net worth statement compares your assets (what you own) and your liabilities (what you owe). Your net worth is the difference between your assets and your liabilities. List your assets at today's prices or current market value. In other words, determine the value on what you could receive if you sold them today, not what you paid for them.

Calculate your net worth once a year. This will help measure your financial progress. After you pull your information together the first time, it will be simple to update each year. An excellent online resource for determining your net worth is provided by CCH Financial Planning at the website www.finance.cch.com/sohoApplets/NetWorth.asp.

Your next step is to review the following checklist. A few of these items are not covered in the scope of this book, but using the resources I've provided can help you explore those topics on your own.

Circle the action steps you've already accomplished, determine which of the remaining action steps you plan to take, and note your anticipated completion date. Or you can create your own additional action steps.

- I have a written inventory of my financial documents.
  O ACCOMPLISHED   O PLAN TO TAKE   DATE: ____/____/____

- I have read and understand all my insurance policies.
  O ACCOMPLISHED   O PLAN TO TAKE   DATE: ____/____/____

- I talk about money and finances with my spouse or partner.
  O ACCOMPLISHED   O PLAN TO TAKE   DATE: ____/____/____

- I have a will, durable power of attorney, and medical directive.
  O ACCOMPLISHED   O PLAN TO TAKE   DATE: ____/____/____

- I know who the beneficiaries are on my life insurance, IRAs, retirement accounts, and U.S. Savings Bonds.
  O ACCOMPLISHED   O PLAN TO TAKE   DATE: ____/____/____

- I have tracked my spending and developed a spending plan.
  O ACCOMPLISHED   O PLAN TO TAKE   DATE: ____/____/____

- I pay all my bills on time each month.
  O ACCOMPLISHED   O PLAN TO TAKE   DATE: ____/____/____

- I pay my credit card bills off each month.
  O ACCOMPLISHED   O PLAN TO TAKE   DATE: ____/____/____

- I have eliminated all my credit card debt.
  O ACCOMPLISHED   O PLAN TO TAKE   DATE: ____/____/____

- I request and review my credit report annually.
  O ACCOMPLISHED   O PLAN TO TAKE   DATE: ____/____/____

- I understand my credit score and how to improve it.
  O ACCOMPLISHED   O PLAN TO TAKE   DATE: ____/____/____

- I have taken steps to protect myself and my family from identity theft.
  O ACCOMPLISHED   O PLAN TO TAKE   DATE: ____/____/____

- I have reviewed my annual Social Security statement.
  O ACCOMPLISHED   O PLAN TO TAKE   DATE: ____/____/____

- I have exercised my opt-out rights to stop the preapproved unsolicited credit card offers
  O ACCOMPLISHED   O PLAN TO TAKE   DATE: ____/___/___

- I have fully established my contingency fund.
  O ACCOMPLISHED   O PLAN TO TAKE   DATE: ____/___/___

- I regularly have money automatically transferred from my paycheck or bank account to an emergency fund.
  O ACCOMPLISHED   O PLAN TO TAKE   DATE: ____/___/___

- I contribute the maximum to my company-sponsored retirement plan.
  O ACCOMPLISHED   O PLAN TO TAKE   DATE: ____/___/___

- I have completed the Ballpark Estimate, a tool to determine if I am saving enough for a financially secure retirement (www.choosetosave.org).
  O ACCOMPLISHED   O PLAN TO TAKE   DATE: ____/___/___

- I have determined my net worth.
  O ACCOMPLISHED   O PLAN TO TAKE   DATE: ____/___/___

NOW IT'S TIME TO PASS IT ON

I hope reading this book has inspired you to achieve financial fitness. Many women have shared their success stories with me, and reading their stories helps motivate us to set our own goals to achieve financial fitness. Why? Because it makes us realize we're not alone on our journey, and no matter how silly or stupid we might feel about a mistake we made, or how bad we feel for taking no action at all, now we know plenty of others have been down that same road—and overcome the same challenges.

Many of the women I've worked with have told me how excited they've been to tell family and friends what they've learned, and how gratifying it is to educate their children about money matters. In some cases it offers hope of breaking generational patterns of poor money management and creating secure futures. Here are some of their experiences.

> ### · PROFIT FROM HER STORY ·
>
> *Cassie* says:
> Find a place to share your knowledge!
>
> "I have seriously started to think about what I can give back. I am planning on getting in touch with my local Women's and Children's Center to see if I can offer some job counseling for women entering the workforce late in life because of divorce, or women returning to the workforce after raising their children."

> ### · PROFIT FROM HER STORY ·
>
> *Leta* says:
> Start your own support group!
>
> "I have started a small support circle of women friends who are dealing with elder-parent situations. We meet once a month, and this is a good outlet and sounding place for all that elder care entails. It's also a good place to discuss how we are going to take care ourselves financially in the future, so that these dilemmas do not fall so hard on our children as we age."

Teaching your children about money

So many people think we should be teaching financial education in our schools, and I couldn't agree more. But I think it's even more important for parents to teach their children about money. Even very young children should have discretionary funds to spend as they see fit. Saving, decision making, planning, sharing, charity, and responsibility are just some of the lessons that can be taught through an allowance.

Have open and honest discussions with your children about money. It's best to begin teaching them financial basics when they start school. Put them on the family payroll by paying them an allowance. If you pay them in cash, don't pay them with a $5, $10, or $20 bill. Instead, pay them with multiple bills—for example, five $1 bills to visually show them how much money goes to savings, charitable donations, and so on. Another idea is to deduct for taxes and Social Security, and show the amount deducted on a pay stub. Teach your children about the importance of regular savings by deducting automatically from their allowance and depositing the amount in a savings account. You can also match their savings deduction to teach them what happens when they contribute to an employer-matching pension plan.

Incorporate their financial education into household chores, grocery shopping, and bill paying by assigning each child the job of determining the weekly menu for the family and making out the grocery list. But don't stop there. Take your kids grocery shopping with you. Give them a calculator, and challenge them to determine how much the groceries cost before they get to the checkout stand. Reward them if their estimate is within $5.

Begin teaching your children about how to use a checkbook register as soon as they can write. Every time they receive money (gifts, allowances, etc.), have them write down the amount in the checkbook register. Each time they use their money to buy something, record their purchase and deduct the amount from their register. Your children will know where they're spending their money, how to use a checkbook register, and the importance of using cash instead of credit cards.

Instead of just giving your children money when they ask, teach them how to work and save for the things they want. One way to do this is to keep a list of chores above and beyond their household duties. Write down each chore with an assigned dollar value. Your children have a way to earn extra money while learning the importance of working and saving for something they want to buy. Too many kids think all they have to do is ask Dad and Mom for money, which gives them a false sense of security and leaves them unprepared for adulthood.

Teach your kids about income taxes by including them in the process. Once you've completed your tax preparation, ask your kids to help you review the information. They can read numbers from your W-2s, 1099s, and other documents. Although it's a long process, it benefits both you and your children. They will probably ask lots of questions, which is a great way to learn. You might also consider rewarding them if you get a tax refund.

· PROFIT FROM HER STORY ·

Jan says:
My sons learned how saving money can really pay off!

"My two teenage sons had to save the money for their car insurance deductible before they were allowed to drive. My husband and I opened a CD in their names, and as long as the kids never have a car accident, the CD will continue to grow. The CD will eventually be theirs when they're out on their own. But if they have a car accident, the deductible will have to be replaced before they can drive again. My seventeen-year-old regularly deposits money into his CD, and he's saved the deductible three to four times over. Our auto insurance gives a good student discount, which we've used to motivate our sons to keep their GPAs high. If they get a 3.5 GPA, we'll pay 50 percent of their car insurance. If they get a 3.75 GPA, we'll pay 75 percent, and if they get a 3.9 or 4.0 GPA, we'll pay 100 percent of their car insurance. It's a win-win situation for everyone."

A reality in today's society is that most people use credit or debit cards to make purchases. They seldom use cash. Educating your children about credit card basics is critical to ensure they don't get themselves into credit card debt when they're out on their own. According to Nellie Mae, the average undergraduate has $2,200 in credit card debt, and 56 percent of undergraduates got their first credit card before age eighteen. One way to teach your teenagers how to use a credit card wisely is to predetermine how much your children will have for clothing, school activities, lunches, and so on, and give them a credit card with a limit of that amount. Task them with the assignment to use their credit responsibly. When the monthly statement comes in, sit down with them, review it, and pay it off. You'll be teaching your kids how to use credit responsibly. I also recommend you have them read Chapter Five and discuss it with them.

· PROFIT FROM HER STORY ·

Beth says:

Involve young adults in family finances!

"So many of us hunger and thirst for the knowledge and don't even realize how hungry and thirsty we are. I shared the experience with friends, coworkers, my boyfriend, and most important, my nineteen-year-old son. We live together. I work full time, and he works part time and goes to college. There has been a chasm between his finances and mine. I was able to sit him down finally and bridge that chasm. We now meet weekly and have a plan to pool our resources and save while he still lives at home."

· PROFIT FROM HER STORY ·

Wanda says:

We need to teach the next generation about money!

"My daughter thinks the same as I do about young people and finance, especially young women. Becky now works as human resources manager for buyers in Macy's corporate offices in San Francisco, and she cannot believe that people can graduate from college with business degrees and still not understand their own pay stubs and W-2s or how to fill out a W-4.

"With Becky, I opened a checking account for her when she was sixteen and had a part-time job. I taught her how to reconcile it and told her I would not bail her out if she was ever overdrawn. The same was true when I signed for a credit card for her when she went to college. I have never had to bail her out for any reason. I am very proud of her skills with money and saving, as well as in investing in retirement for her and Brad. Becky still has the same credit card she had in college but without my name attached to it.

"I see a lot of women who are not money wise until something tragic happens in their lives that forces them to learn. I have always thought that the generation of my daughter would somehow be more educated and independent, because that is what I did with my daughter, but this is just not true. Basically, what I hear is either 'Mom and Dad will foot the bill,' or 'No problem,' or 'I will inherit Mom and Dad's money.' I have for many years thought that there should be some sort of basic finance class required in high school. I have young people come into my office to explain their paycheck to them!"

Nora says:
I had to use tough love when it came to
my kids and money—but it paid off!

"My child challenge is that Justin was draining me of money, because he was not being responsible with his money while in his first year of college. So one of my challenges was: How do I support my child but still take care of myself? I spent a long time with this, and I struggled with it. I still struggle with it. If I do not teach my children to be responsible—and lead by example—who will? Although it has been very difficult for me—and for Justin—I set limits. And I did not give him the money he decided he needed and wanted at my expense.

"I think most parents believe they owe their children, because their children are the consequence of a decision they made. But I'm now of the firm opinion that that is just not so.

"While Justin's lessons have been painful for both him and for me, the upside is that Ashley, his younger sister, is learning from his mistakes and experiences. Not that she won't make mistakes of her own—she will. But one of the decisions she made was to live at home, to find a job this summer, and to go to community college. She sees that this will take some burden away from me (her father will not be assisting her with tuition or making any financial contribution to her college education) and that it will teach her responsibility. Sure, she won't be able to live on her own in an apartment, but she will also be able to save for college and acquire some of the things that her brother has not been able to acquire.

"As a reward for this, I am matching whatever funds she saves. So there is an incentive for her to save money for the next two years of college. I have an ulterior motive: I want her to see the

▶

benefit of saving money from her paycheck and investing in her company's 401(k) plan—especially if it matches funds. I'm hoping she will see the value of paying herself first and saving, and that it can be done in one step. So far, she has agreed to this.

"I guess you could say that I've learned to practice what I preach. And I do not see myself as a terrible mother. I am a good mother. I'm teaching them a lesson in a much kinder and gentler way than the world at large would be willing to teach that lesson to my children (had I chosen to continue on the path of least resistance), which was not responsible from either a financial or a parenting perspective.

"And it does get easier with practice. Sure, the kids resisted. Sure, I have doubts. But I've learned to 'go with my gut' and to tell the truth: I can't afford to invest in irresponsibility. I must take care of myself first. I'm generous and willing to share, but only if they are willing to be good stewards of the resources I share with them. If they are unwilling to be good stewards of their resources, I must withdraw my support of that decision. Otherwise, I would be a poor steward of my own resources. And how could I ever demand they be good stewards while I was a poor one?

"And tough love does pay: I was able to make the first $3,000 contribution to my very own Roth IRA for last year and saved $1,000 for my Financial Freedom account. I could have bailed Justin out, but I listened to the voice of reason."

Mary Jo is a star student and has made enormous strides in taking control of her money after ending a thirty-year marriage. In addition, she's teaching her fourteen-year-old son about finances. She's taken him to a class on checking accounts, opened his own checking account, and developed a spending plan for him.

· PROFIT FROM HER STORY ·

Mary Jo says:
I'm so proud of how my son manages his money!

"When I left my marriage, I had no idea how to manage money. Heck, I didn't know what money really was. My paycheck went to my husband, and he planned what to do, down to the last penny. I earned good money and knew that was my job—to continue being a paycheck. After thirty years of marriage, we didn't have a savings account, didn't have CDs, bonds, stocks, and so on. Just a huge pile of debt. I realize now that debt was my husband's way of controlling me. In the last three years, I have paid off that debt—more than $50,000 on credit cards. I have paid for a divorce ($16,000) and have savings, CDs, stocks, and IRAs. I've invested in 529 educational savings accounts and guaranteed education tuition (GET) accounts for Joey and four of my grandchildren. I have savings bonds and help my mother, children, grandchildren, and blind aunt, who is seventy years old and raising three grandchildren. I learned to overcome my fear of being too stupid to handle money. I've learned to respect it and to use it (I hope wisely most of the time). I have learned to take care of myself with insurance and a will.

"In the early days I was really good about saving change and dollar bills. It took me awhile to graduate to effectively handling a whole paycheck. I was afraid of the larger sums and had to learn to budget. I am constantly surprised by how much I enjoy reading and learning about money. The language of money is not at all as difficult as learning to cook (stocks versus braised meat). And yet I ignored it for fifty years.

"Joey and I attended the Varsity Checking class at Kitsap Federal Credit Union, and it was wonderful. I learned several things about writing checks, including ways to prevent check fraud.

▶

▶

Joey receives an allowance, and out of that he manages his own checking account, investments, and buys what he needs.

"We met with a financial adviser, and Joey set up both a 529 educational savings account (that he funds with his dad's Social Security—$176 per month) and a separate account that he can play around with in the stock market ($60) a month. Then we met with another financial adviser several weeks ago, and she is going to include Joey in some classes she has for teens.

"Joey also manages and runs his own business as a distributor for mini-motorcycles. He has ups and downs with that, as the amount of time he can dedicate is controlled by his schoolwork. But it is an excellent opportunity for him, and he has learned a lot about marketing, selling, and managing, and he has many big ideas.

"The biggest lesson that I see he has learned during the last year is being smart about buying games and movies. They were taking *all* of his money until he learned to trade and bargain and look past Wal-Mart. Joey also calculates out loud how many hours of work it takes to buy something. He thinks he will start out earning $10 per hour and uses that to figure."

I hope you found these stories inspiring and will find ways in your own life to pass along your newly earned financial wisdom. And remember, like learning a foreign language, educating yourself about money is an ongoing process—taking control and learning about money and finances won't happen by attending one class, seminar, or reading one book. But the journey can also be fun! Congratulations. You're well on your way to getting your financial house in spotless order!

I always love to hear from readers, so if you have a story of your own you'd like to share, please email me through my website: www.moneywisewomen.net or www.marciabrixey.com.

Whatever you think you can do or believe you can do, begin it. Action has magic, grace and power in it.

—Goethe

Money Wi$e Women Action Steps

DETERMINE YOUR GOALS AND WRITE AN ACTION PLAN

This is a summary of all the action steps I've listed throughout the book. I put them all in one list so you could see the whole scope of possible actions. But don't get overwhelmed! Just pick one and do that. Then go on to the next one.

Develop a spending and debt reduction plan:

- Track your spending for thirty days. Whenever you spend money, write down how much you spent and what you spent it on.

- Ask yourself: *Would I buy this item if I were paying cash?*

- Shop only when you need something.

- Before you buy anything that costs more than $100, wait twenty-four hours.

- Carry the checkout checklist in your wallet. Review it before buying anything.

- Plan your purchases. Never shop for recreation.

- Set money limits before you go shopping.

- Make a commitment and set goals to become debt free.

- Decide not to incur any more debt.

- Summarize your credit card debt.

- Never carry your credit card unless you plan to use it.

- Accelerate your credit card payments. Make more than the minimum payment on your credit cards.

- Call your creditors to request a lower interest rate.

- Get a credit card with no annual fee and a low interest rate.

- Get a credit card in your name only.

- Ask your credit card company to waive any annual fees.

- Investigate and consider transferring balances from accounts with higher interest rates to accounts with lower interest rates.

- Read the fine print on your credit card accounts.

Develop a savings and investment plan:

- Always pay yourself first.

- Review your W-4 form. You may be able to increase your take-home pay. Use the extra cash to fund your emergency account, contingency account, pension plan, or IRA.

- Set aside a percentage of each paycheck for savings.

- Open an emergency account. Strive to have a balance of three to six months' worth of living expenses.

- Open a contingency account for your unexpected or irregular expenses—for example, car repairs, home repairs, vet bills, and so on.

- Make your savings and investments automatic. Use payroll deduction or have the money regularly withheld from your bank account.

- Increase your savings whenever you get a raise, cost of living increase, or other unexpected cash.

- Save your change each day. At the end of a month, open a savings account.

- Buy U.S. Savings Bonds. You can buy savings bonds through payroll deduction or online at www.treasurydirect.gov.

- Reduce your mortgage payments by refinancing.

- If you carry private mortgage insurance (PMI), make sure you really need it or ask your lender to drop it.

- Understand the magic of compounding interest. It's best to start investing at an early age, but it's never too late to start! Share this information with your spouse and children.

- Complete a savings-need calculation to determine whether you're saving enough annually for a comfortable retirement. Use the Ballpark Estimate, which is available online at www.choosetosave.org.

- Educate yourself on mutual funds and open an account.

Learn more about Social Security and plan for your retirement:

- Review your Social Security statement for accuracy and make the necessary corrections.

- Request your Social Security statement (if you don't have it) online at www.socialsecurity.gov or call (800) 772-1213.

- Complete the online calculator to estimate your potential Social Security retirement benefit. Visit www.socialsecurity.gov.

- If you change your name, complete the necessary paperwork with the Social Security Administration.

- Participate in your employer's pension plan. If you can't afford to contribute the maximum, start small, but participate!

- Educate yourself on the different investment options in your 401(k) or 403(b).

- Review all pension options available to you when your spouse retires. For more information, visit the Women's Institute for a Secure Retirement at www.wiser.heinz.org.

- Open and fund an individual retirement account (IRA).

- If you don't work outside the home, have your husband open and contribute to a spousal IRA for you.

Request your credit report and improve your credit score:

- Request your free credit report annually from all three credit-reporting agencies at www.annualcreditreport.com.

- Review your credit report for errors.

- Correct any errors on your credit report(s) and follow up to ensure the corrections have been made.

- Request your credit score, and if necessary, determine which actions you must take to improve your score.

- Understand what your liability is for joint accounts at the time of divorce or death.

- Pay your bills consistently on time.

- Keep your debt reasonable. Your account balances should be below 75 percent of your available credit.

- Avoid too many hard inquiries. They can be interpreted as a sign you're seeking credit and may be in financial difficulty.

Minimize your risk of identity theft:

- Give your Social Security number only to those who need it.

- Ask these questions: Why do you need it? How will it be used? How do you protect it from being stolen? What will happen if I don't give it to you?

- Don't carry your Social Security card (or the cards of other family members) in your purse or wallet.

- Never have your Social Security number or driver's license number preprinted on your checks.

- Make a photocopy of the contents of your wallet.

- Shred credit card receipts and any other sensitive documents before you throw them away.

- Follow up with creditors if your bills and bank statements don't arrive on time.

- Install a locked mailbox or have your mail delivered to a post office box.

- Don't leave unwanted blank credit applications in your mailbox.

- Keep unsolicited, preapproved credit card applications out of your mail by exercising your opt-out rights. Call (888) 567-8688 or visit www.optoutprescreen.com. You'll need to provide your Social Security number.

- Reduce your junk mail by registering at the Direct Marketing Association website at www.dmaconsumers.org/consumerassistance.html.

- Reduce the number of unsolicited telemarketing phone calls by registering your phone number at www.donotcall.gov.

- Password-protect your computer to prevent access by unauthorized people.

- Install a firewall to limit uninvited access to your computer.

- Stop opening email attachments from people you don't know.

- If you think you are a victim of identity theft, call the Identity Theft Hotline at (877) 438-4338.

Protect yourself, your family, and the things you love:

- Review your automobile and homeowners insurance deductibles. Raising deductibles can reduce your premiums by up to 20 percent.

- Review your life and disability insurance to ensure you have adequate coverage.

- Investigate and consider buying long-term care insurance.

- Make an appointment with an attorney to write a will to protect your family.

- Prepare a durable power of attorney and advance healthcare directive.

- Write a letter to your family providing them all the information they will need if you die or become incapacitated.

- Complete the funeral planning form found online at www.peoples-memorial.org.

- Review your nonprobate assets (life insurance, pension plans, IRAs, etc.) to ensure you have named the appropriate beneficiary.

- Complete a household inventory.

- Talk to your family about being prepared for a disaster.

- Make emergency contact cards for everyone in your family.

- Get an evacuation box to protect your financial paperwork.

Learn more about financial fitness:

- Get a money buddy—someone to learn about money with who will hold you accountable.

- Take a class or workshop.

- Attend a financial conference.

- Read a book about money or finance.

- Join or start a book club.

- Join or start an investment club.

- Study financial websites.

- Subscribe to an online financial newsletter.

- Learn more about your rights as a widow, divorced spouse, or spouse.

- Make an appointment with a financial adviser or certified financial planner.

- Read the Money Wi$e Women blog at www.moneywise womenblog.net.

MONTHLY SPENDING PLAN SUMMARY

MONTHLY EXPENSES	PROJECTED SPENDING	ACTUAL SPENDING	YOUR GOALS
SHELTER			
Mortgage/Rent			
Property Taxes			
Electricity			
Gas/Propane			
Wood			
Water			
Sewer			
Garbage			
Cable TV			
Internet Service			
House Cleaner			
Gardener			
Home and Yard Maintenance			
Home Furnishings			
Home Improvement Projects			
Other			
PHONE			
Basic Service			
Long Distance			
Cell/Pager			
Other			
TRANSPORTATION			
Car Payment(s)			
Registrations			
Public Transportation			
Parking			

MONTHLY EXPENSES	PROJECTED SPENDING	ACTUAL SPENDING	YOUR GOALS
TRANSPORTATION (continued)			
Car Repair and Maintenance			
Other			
FOOD			
Groceries			
School Lunches			
Work Lunches			
Coffee Breaks			
Snacks			
Restaurants and Takeout			
INSURANCE			
Auto			
Homeowners/Renters			
Medical			
Life			
Disability			
Other			
CHILDREN			
Daycare/Baby Sitters			
School Expenses			
Toys			
Allowances			
Child Support			
Extra Activities (lessons, tutors, etc.)			
Other			
CLOTHING			
Self			
Spouse			
Children			

MONTHLY EXPENSES	PROJECTED SPENDING	ACTUAL SPENDING	YOUR GOALS
CLOTHING (continued)			
Laundry/Dry Cleaning			
Other			
MEDICAL			
Doctor			
Dentist			
Medical Deductible and Copayments			
Drugs and Prescriptions			
Glasses and Contacts			
Therapy			
Other			
PERSONAL			
Hair Stylist			
Manicure			
Massage			
Cosmetics			
Other			
PETS			
Pet Food and Supplies			
Veterinary Care			
Other			
ENTERTAINMENT			
Movies, Plays, Concerts, etc.			
Video Rentals			
Spectator Sports			
Golf, Softball, Fishing, Boating, Bowling, etc.			
Club Dues and Memberships			

MONTHLY EXPENSES	PROJECTED SPENDING	ACTUAL SPENDING	YOUR GOALS
ENTERTAINMENT (continued)			
Health Club or Gym			
Crafts and Hobbies			
Vacations/Travel			
Other			
DONATIONS			
Church			
Charities			
Other			
DEBT			
Credit Card(s)			
Installment Loan(s)			
Student Loan(s)			
Other			
GIFTS AND HOLIDAYS			
Birthdays			
Anniversaries and Weddings			
Holidays			
Other			
HIGHER EDUCATION			
Tuition			
Books			
Student Housing			
Other			
MISCELLANEOUS			
Alimony			
Newspapers			
Magazines			
Books			

MONTHLY EXPENSES	PROJECTED SPENDING	ACTUAL SPENDING	YOUR GOALS
MISCELLANEOUS (continued)			
CDs, Tapes, and Videos			
Computer Expenses			
Postage			
Occupational Fees, Licenses, Dues			
Cigarettes			
Alcohol			
SAVINGS AND INVESTMENTS			
Savings Account(s)			
IRA(s)			
U.S. Savings Bonds			
Mutual Funds			
Money Market Account(s)			
Investment Property			

INVENTORY OF ASSETS AND LIABILITIES

Banks and Credit Unions

INSTITUTION CONTACT INFO	ACCOUNT OWNERS	ACCOUNT # AND TYPE	CURRENT BALANCE
TOTAL			

Other Investments (Certificates of Deposit, Treasury Bills, Notes, Bonds, etc.)

INSTITUTION CONTACT INFO	TYPE OF INVESTMENT	AMOUNT/ INTEREST RATE	MATURITY DATE
TOTAL			

Mutual Funds and Brokerage Accounts

NAME/ADDRESS/ PHONE	ACCOUNT OWNERS	# OF SHARES/ MARKET VALUE	PURCHASE DATE
TOTAL			

Stocks

NAME	OWNERS	# OF SHARES/ MARKET VALUE	PURCHASE DATE
TOTAL			

Annuities

COMPANY CONTACT INFO	ANNUITANT OWNER	APPROXIMATE MARKET VALUE	PURCHASE DATE
TOTAL			

Savings Bonds

TYPE (EE, I, etc.)	SERIAL NUMBER	FACE VALUE	PURCHASE DATE
TOTAL			

Retirement Plans—401(k), 403(b), 457, IRAs, SIMPLE Plans, and so on—for Both You and Your Spouse

COMPANY CONTACT INFO	TYPE OF PLAN	APPROXIMATE VALUE	% YOU CONTRIBUTE
YOU			
YOUR SPOUSE			

Real Estate

Monthly rent amount $_____

Monthly mortgage amount $_____

Mortgage company _____

Loan # _____

Address _____

Phone _____

Mortgage balance $_____ Length of loan _____

Interest rate _____ Fixed or variable _____

How is your home held? (e.g., joint tenancy) _____

Second Home:

Monthly mortgage amount $_____

Mortgage company _____

Loan # _____

Address _____

Phone _____

Mortgage balance $_____ Length of loan _____

Interest rate _____ Fixed or variable _____

Credit Card Debt

COMPANY CONTACT INFO	ACCOUNT NUMBER	BALANCE DUE	INTEREST RATE
TOTAL			

Student Loans

SCHOOL/ UNIVERSITY	ADDRESS/ PHONE	BALANCE DUE	INTEREST RATE
TOTAL			

Auto/Boat Loans

VEHICLE	LENDER CONTACT INFO	INTEREST RATE/ TERM	BALANCE DUE
TOTAL			

Monthly Income

Your monthly income $_____

Spouse's monthly income $_____

OTHER TYPES OF INCOME	MONTHLY AMOUNT
TOTAL	

Insurance (Life Insurance, Disability Insurance, Long-Term Care Insurance)

COMPANY CONTACT INFO	TYPE/ AMOUNT	POLICY #	BENEFICIARY
TOTAL			

Other Insurance (Auto, Homeowners, Liability, etc.)

INSURANCE COMPANY	ADDRESS/ PHONE	TYPE OF INSURANCE	POLICY #

Estate Planning

Do you have a will or living trust?   O YES   O NO

Attorney's name_____

Address_____

Phone_____

Where do you keep your will?_____

Do you have durable power of attorney?   O YES   O NO

· RESOURCES ·

Financial and Motivational Resource Books

Smart Women Finish Rich, by David Bach

Start Late, Finish Rich, by David Bach

The Automatic Millionaire, by David Bach

The Finish Rich Workbook, by David Bach

It's More Than Money—It's Your Life, by Candace Bahr and Ginita Wall

Think $ingle! The Woman's Guide to Financial Security at Every Stage of Life, by Janet Bodnar

If Life Is a Game, These Are the Rules, by Cherie Carter-Scott

A Deep Breath of Life, by Alan Cohen

Nice Girls Don't Get Rich: 75 Avoidable Mistakes Women Make with Money, by Lois P. Frankel

Creating True Prosperity, by Shakti Gawain

Creative Visualization: Using the Power of Your Imagination to Create What You Want in Your Life, by Shakti Gawain

Debt Proof Living, by Mary Hunt

The Financially Confident Woman, by Mary Hunt

Zero Debt, by Lynnette Khalfani

Rich Dad, Poor Dad, by Robert Kiyosaki

The Runway of Life, by Peter Legge

Wake-Up Calls, by Joan Lunden

Learn to Be an Optimist: A Practical Guide to Achieving Happiness, by Lucy MacDonald

Money Harmony: Resolving Money Conflicts in Your Life and Relationships, by Olivia Mellon

The Energy of Money: A Spiritual Guide to Financial and Personal Fulfillment, by Maria Nemeth, PhD

Saving on a Shoestring, by Barbara O'Neill

The Nine Steps to Financial Freedom, by Suze Orman

The Road to Wealth, by Suze Orman

Women and Money, by Suze Orman

What's Next? Women Redefining Their Dreams in the Prime of Life, by Rena Pederson

Choosing Joy, Creating Abundance, by Ellen Peterson

Caring for Your Soul in Matters of Money, by Karen Ramsey

Think Again: New Money Choices, Old Money Myths, by Karen Ramsey

Creating Money: Keys to Abundance, by Sanaya Roman and Duane Packer

The Four Agreements, by Don Miguel Ruize

The Money Mystique, by Karen Sheridan

Overcoming Underearning: Overcome Your Money Fears and Earn What You Deserve, by Barbara Stanny

Prince Charming Isn't Coming: How Women Get Smart about Money, by Barbara Stanny

Secrets of Six-Figure Women: Surprising Strategies to Up Your Earnings and Change Your Life, by Barbara Stanny

Why Women Earn Le$$: How to Make What You're Really Worth, by Mikelann Valterra

You'll find reviews of all these books and links to buy them on my website, at www.moneywisewomen.net.

Resource Websites

For your convenience, all of these websites are linked on my website (www.moneywisewomen.net or www.marciabrixey.com), along with the latest additions.

American Savings Education Council—www.asec.org

Annual Credit Report—www.annualcreditreport.com

Bankrate.com—www.bankrate.com

Barbara Stanny—www.barbarastanny.com

www.cardratings.com

CNN Money—www.money.cnn.com

Do Not Call Registry—www.ftc.gov/donotcall

Federal Trade Commission—www.ftc.gov

Fight Identity Theft—www.fightidentitytheft.com

Financial Recovery Institute—www.financialrecovery.com

FindLegalForms.com—www.findlegalforms.com

First Government—www.firstgov.gov

Hayek Services—www.hayek-services.com

Identity Theft Center—www.idtheftcenter.org

JumpStart—www.jumpstart.org

Legacy Writer—www.legacywriter.com

LegalZoom.com—www.legalzoom.com

Money Wi$e Women—www.moneywisewomen.net

Money Wise Women Blog—www.moneywisewomenblog.net

Morningstar—www.morningstar.com

Motley Fool—www.fool.com

My Money—www.mymoney.gov

National Association of Investor Clubs—www.betterinvesting.org

National Endowment Foundation for Education—www.nefe.org

Nolo.com—www.nolo.com

Opt-Out—www.optoutprescreen.com

People's Memorial Association—www.peoples-memorial.org

Privacy Rights Clearinghouse—www.privacyrights.org

Social Security Administration—www.socialsecurity.gov

360 Degrees of Financial Literacy—www.360financialliteracy.org

Truth about Credit—www.truthaboutcredit.org

U.S. Savings Bonds—www.savingsbond.gov

Wi$e Up—www.wiseupwomen.org

Women's Earning Institute—www.womenearning.com

Women's Institute for Financial Education—www.wife.org

Women's Institute for a Secure Retirement—www.wiser.heinz.org

· ACKNOWLEDGMENTS ·

From the bottom of my heart, thank you to all the women who so willingly and honestly shared their stories of challenges and successes. I know the women who read this book will relate to your stories, and they will know they are not alone. Thank you!

Thank you to my parents, Henry and Betty, for teaching me to follow my heart and passion; for always telling me I could do anything I made up my mind to do, and to never give up.

My husband, Steve, is my partner and greatest supporter. He's been behind me with my book and all my Money Wise Women activities. Thank you, Steve, for your never-ending support, and for the countless hours you spent reading and editing my work.

· ABOUT THE AUTHOR ·

Marcia Brixey is the founder and president of Money Wise Women Educational Services, a nonprofit organization that hosts Money Wi$e Women Forums. Marcia is passionate about educating and empowering women to achieve financial fitness.

Marcia's work and lifetime experiences enable her to share a wealth of financial insight. She was inspired to take early retirement from her public relations job with the Social Security Administration in August 2002 after reading the quote, "Our purpose in life is to find our gift, perfect it, and give it back to others." Her twenty-six years of experience with the Social Security Administration includes posts as district manager, supervisor, and public relations specialist. She graduated from California State University, East Bay, with a BS in Business Administration. Marcia's enthusiasm, passion, and down-to-earth approach inspire her audiences to take action. Today she hosts Money Wi$e Women Forums throughout the western United States.

Marcia has been the featured speaker at numerous conferences and meetings, including the Prudential Financial Stepping Out Conference in Santa Clara, California and Chicago; Choice Hotels Convention in Orlando, Florida; Invest in Yourself Strategies for Women Conference in Costa Mesa, California; Women and Money Conference in Bellingham, Washington; Northwest Women's Show in Seattle, Washington and Portland, Oregon; Clemson University

Professional Women's Conference in Seattle and Portland; Women at Work and Play Conference in Portland; and eWomenNetwork meetings and Staples Small Business Events in the Seattle metropolitan area. She has also been a guest lecturer onboard Celebrity Cruise Lines. Marcia is a member of the National Speaker's Association.

Marcia is a former columnist for *The Kitsap Sun* newspaper, which serves the Kitsap Peninsula in western Washington. She has been a guest on *Northwest Afternoon* (Seattle, KOMO TV), *About the Money* (Seattle, KCTS TV), and *Good Day Sacramento* (Sacramento, KMAX TV), and she is a regular guest on KING TV *Morning News* (Seattle, NBC affiliate) and the Q13 *Morning News* (Seattle, FOX TV). Marcia has been interviewed on radio stations KYPT 96.5 FM, Seattle; KKNW 1150 AM, Seattle; and WOND 1400 AM, in Atlantic City, New Jersey; and she was host of a weekly talk radio show, "Let's Talk About Money," in 2004. She's a mentor for the Department of Labor Women's Bureau Wi$e Up Women program, and she received the 2006 YWCA Woman of Achievement award in Kitsap County.

You can reach Marcia at:

P.O. Box 2508

Silverdale, WA 98383

marcia@marciabrixey.com

www.marciabrixey.com

www.moneywisewomen.net